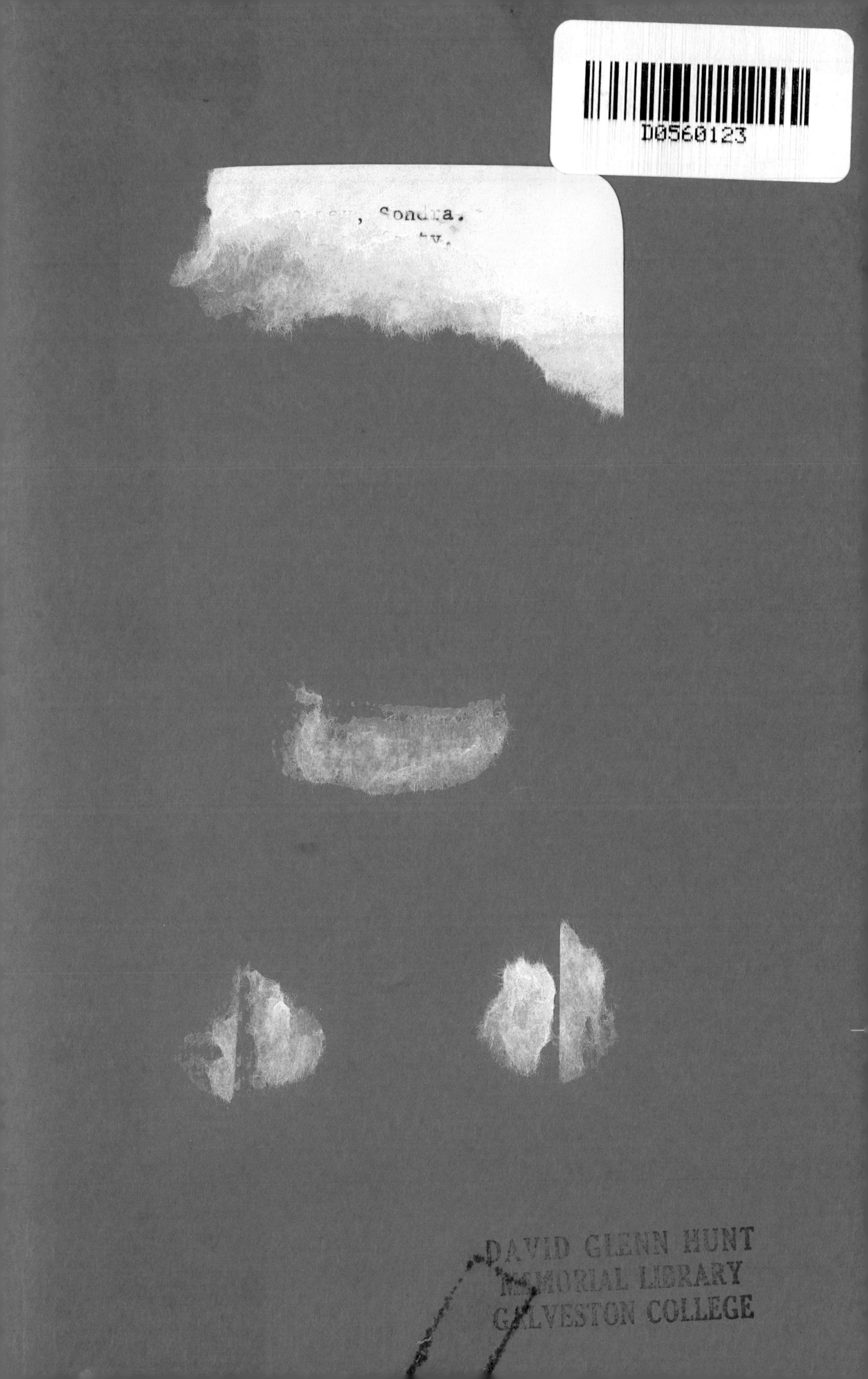

AFTER FORTY

Books by Claire Cox

The New-Time Religion

The Upbeat Generation

How Women Can Make Up to
$1000 a Week in Direct Selling

The Fourth R—What Can Be Taught
About Religion in the Public Schools

Parents on Trial (WITH DAVID WILKERSON)

Choose Success (WITH BILLY B. SHARP)

Faces People Wear (WITH CHARLES DISALVO)

How To Beat the High Cost of College

Sondra Gorney
and
Claire Cox

AFTER FORTY

How Women Can Achieve Fulfillment

THE DIAL PRESS NEW YORK 1973

Library of Congress Cataloging in Publication Data

Gorney, Sondra.
After forty.

Bibliography: p.
1. Women in the United States. 2. Middle age.
3. Women—Conduct of life. I. Cox, Claire, joint author. II. Title.
HQ1420.G66 301.41'2 72-13463

Designed by Judith Lerner Thiesen
Printed in the United States of America
Second Printing, 1973

Dedication

To our husbands,
Jay Gorney and Max Lowenthal,
whose editorial comment,
patience, understanding,
encouragement, wit, and love
made this joint venture possible.
Without them,
we could not hope
to achieve the maturity
for which we strive.

Contents

Preface

"THE WORLD SEEMS to be falling in on me," an attractive mature woman confided. "I just took my mother to the hospital. I'm worried about my son's draft status. My husband needs a job. And *I* have to complete a term paper. It seems that I've had nothing but pressure from all sides for the past forty years. God knows what the next forty will be like!"

Another woman commented: "I was trying on a midi-skirt and then I saw myself in a three-way mirror. How did I ever get to looking so old and fat?"

And a third lamented: "Now that the kids are away at college, I just don't know what to do with myself."

These concerns and many others like them have been expressed during personal encounters with the over-forty housewife, divorcée, widow, "bachelor girl," and even the seemingly contented career woman. So many have discussed the problems of their mature years with us that it is apparent that a significant number—if not most—women past forty are facing problems in adjusting to their lives, particularly in our youth-oriented society, where to be young is to be beautiful. Whether their concerns are physical aches and pains, social ineptness, or mental lethargy, something obviously has been bugging many of the mature women we hear from and meet.

On the brighter side, we also have encountered dynamic, productive middle-aged women who populate every field of professional endeavor. They include actresses, physicians, lawyers, designers, social workers, marriage counselors, professors, and businesswomen—among them secretaries, stenographers, bookkeepers, and executives.

There are thousands of women who are happy doing their "own thing," whether it be filling a nine-to-five office job or running a household. But even they may feel the need for a boost now and then or a suggestion as to how they might change something about themselves or improve on nature.

In our many encounters, personal and by mail, and in our reading, we found a challenge to try to learn the secrets of the women who have achieved a degree of success and then pass them along to those who need help in solving their individual problems. It is one thing for the high-school girl or college graduate to survey the scene and plan what she thinks she wants to do with her future. But for the woman who has lived at least half her life, the project can be more formidable.

Granted, there are forces outside ourselves that hinder our development; responsibilities, discrimination, intimidation by the youth cult all must be reckoned with at one time or another. How have some women learned to buck discrimination, to work out smooth human relations, and to find their true worth? What can we learn from them?

We started the task of writing this book aware of one relatively new advantage. Women today have a priceless gift—longevity. That means we have more time in which to remedy long-standing errors, recall past experiences, and set new goals. The words of the poet who said "It's never too late" give us promise because of our added years.

It is never too soon, either, for those of us over forty. As two women plunging headlong through middle age, we became involved in our search for personal answers. We, too, wanted advice and guidance to enrich our own lives, and much of what we have learned in our research has provided just that. In the course of our study, we interviewed hundreds of women, both professionals and stay-at-homes. We learned from every one of them.

Our research also led us to the discovery that millions of words have been written about middle age in textbooks, guidebooks, personal stories, even fiction. Much of it we have read, at least in part. Our aim was to extract the meat and condense and highlight only what emphasized the fears—real and imagined—and encouraged acceptance of the positive aspects of the second half of a woman's life.

We consulted a number of men and women specialists in the fields of human behavior and medicine. Their keen observations about the distaff strengths and weaknesses—biological, psychological, and social—added to our understanding of the problems and potentials of mature women.

Here, then, is a guide to feminine fulfillment in the second forty years of life. We hope it provides ways in which you can overcome—or at least minimize—the fears and doubts that confront you. While life may not begin at forty, it *can* begin to be better and, indeed, provide the best years of all!

SONDRA GORNEY

CLAIRE COX

AFTER FORTY

CHAPTER

1

"You're Not Getting Older, You're Getting Better"

THE AUDIENCE cheered when the petite, shapely actress came on stage flashing her famous smile and her flawless legs. When the final curtain dropped, the men in the audience gave a standing ovation to this newest of Broadway stars, and many of them rushed to the stage door clamoring for her autograph. In the days that followed, fan letters poured in asking for photographs and congratulating her on her performance.

Such an accolade is usually accorded to rising young stars on the occasion of their first big hits, but the object of adulation on this evening was a fifty-one-year-old grandmother—Betty Grable, Hollywood's top box-office attraction of the 1940s and pinup queen of the GIs who fought World War II. Miss Grable had just made her opening-night appearance in one of the all-time hit musicals, *Hello, Dolly!* In the audience were some of the 1,500,000 former servicemen who had tacked her picture on barracks room walls and in footlockers when they were GIs

—and some of the sons of the former fighting men were there to cheer, too.

In a country where youth is often glorified, there is still something appealing about countless women who have crossed the great divide of forty and still have the spirit —and appearance—of youth. This is particularly true in the theatrical world. In one past Broadway season alone, the brightest stars of the biggest shows were Katharine Hepburn, sixty; Lauren Bacall, forty-five; Ethel Merman, sixty-one; Zsa Zsa Gabor, forty-seven; Shirley Booth, sixty-one; Shelley Winters, forty-seven; Celeste Holm, fifty; and June Allyson, forty-six. The year before, Julie Harris, then forty-five, packed them in to see a play in which she portrayed a middle-aged woman in love with a young man; and in the winter of 1970, Ruby Keeler, slim and youthful at sixty, came out of retirement to kick up her heels through a revival of *No, No, Nanette,* a hit of the 1920s. The audience roared its approval and admiration.

Although Miss Keeler's was a hard act to follow, Alexis Smith, at fifty, co-starred in the musical *Follies* and won the accolade of being on the cover of *Time* magazine, with a shapely leg kicking high.

What does all this prove? In the words of the TV commercial, "You're not getting older, you're getting better!" It is evident that beauty, charm, talent, wit, abundant energy—and even glamor and sex appeal—need not be the exclusive property of the young female, and that men admire women who can turn middle age into the prime time of their lives. A gallant seventy-one-year-old Frenchman, Jean-Baptiste Trosgros, operator of a highly rated restaurant in Roanne, took the part of the "mature" woman when he was asked what he regarded as the best age of a woman. "I see women of fifty or sixty who are nuggets of gold," he observed, "still coquette, not faded, free, ready to be of service. From thirty-five to forty-five, women are old, and at forty-five the devil takes over and they're beautiful, splendid, maternal, proud. The acidities are gone, and in their place reigns calm. They are worth going out to find, and because of them, some men never grow old. When I see them, my mouth waters."

Whether she is going to be such a "delicacy" is in large part up to the woman herself, for women are often to blame when they find themselves relegated to the sidelines as they move into and through what we call middle age. To some the big number forty stands out like a beacon as a symbol of faded youth, of lost opportunities, of life not really lived, and as an invitation to quietly and gracefully fade away. You do not have to listen to the siren call to sing the menopause blues, however; the increasing number of women who are becoming business executives, rising to the top in elected and appointed political office, and leading the volunteer movement are proof that middle age can be accompanied by beautiful music.

Typical of one predominant attitude—or nonattitude—toward the second forty was the response of the late Aline Saarinen, an attractive television personality, when she was approached with a suggestion for a discussion about women's middle years on her NBC-TV forum "For Women Only." Mrs. Saarinen's first reaction—a natural one for her—was reported to have been, "But why should *that* be a problem?" She went ahead with the program anyway, and after hearing what a few experts had to say and the questions that were posed by the studio audience, she acknowledged that middle age *could* indeed be a real psychological hazard to those who are unaware of the potentialities of life in the mature years. That it had not occurred to her to think of herself as middle-aged was a tribute to the adjustments she had made in her own life.

"We've built our own traps in this country," says Dr. Herbert Spiegel, a psychiatrist on the staff of the Columbia College of Physicians and Surgeons. "The idea that forty-plus is attractive is a foreign idea to many

American women. We're hooked by a concept that paralyzes us . . . and we have to resolve the misunderstanding. At forty one should think of beginning a freer, more mature life. It is a time to revise even precious beliefs that have been held for a long time—a time to be open to new information."

Indeed, for those who face changes in their lives, middle age does not have to be muddle age, the back forty instead of the best forty. There is no reason why it need be a time of crisis accompanied by the "shattering" reality that one is not going to do some of the things one always thought one would. It should be a time of newfound freedom, when children have grown and left home, giving their parents a chance to start over, if not to take a new tack. Dr. Sherwin A. Kaufman, an obstetrician and gynecologist, says that while some women fear they face an end to desirability as women, the psychologically healthy middle-aged woman takes a positive view of her future. "If she reflects on the past," he maintains, "she reflects on her successes—not her failures. She finds pleasure in her family, her friends, her pursuits. She enjoys life."

One of the most difficult aspects of middle age, for men as well as for women, is the fact that some elements of our society persist in overrating youth and devaluing maturity. Writing in the *Medical Tribune,* Dr. Gene L. Usdin, associate professor of clinical psychiatry at the Louisiana State University School of Medicine, noted that middle age has been accepted by nearly every earlier period as the ideal and as the source of leadership. Now, he added, there are those who feel that to be mature is to be "square." Men such as Winston Churchill, Franklin D. Roosevelt, and Dwight D. Eisenhower are looked upon these days as unusual, he contends.

Usdin might have included the distaff side of public life, too—the Eleanor Roosevelts, the Margaret Chase Smiths, the Helen Hayeses, the Pearl Bucks, the Margaret Meads, the Anna Rosenbergs, and many others, including the over-forty women who were elected to Congress in 1970 and 1972, one of them winning the seat that had been vacated by the long-time House majority leader, John McCormack.

The acceptance of women, most of them past forty, in public life says something about how far civilization has come in the last fifty years, particularly in view of the fact that women of mature age head the governments of three nations—India, Israel, and Ceylon. At home, women are becoming active at every level of politics, whereas in times past they had to content themselves with nagging male legislators through such organizations as the League of Women Voters, the PTA, and, alas, the temperance movement, which, largely female in membership, helped push the Volstead Act, which was responsible for the turbulent, lawless years of Prohibition—eventually overwhelmingly decreed to have been a socially costly mistake. Working within established political structures, women—black and white—are serving in city, state, and federal government in elective and appointive posts, as administrators, judges, and legislators. Of course, their status could and should be improved—and it will be, particularly with enactment of the Equal Rights Amendment to the Constitution. Some men still tend to denigrate women in politics and in business, and in the professions, too, but tremendous progress has been made since Great-grandma donned black bloomers and pedaled her bicycle up Fifth Avenue in her campaign for the right to vote.

The examples set by women achievers and the determined campaign of the women's liberation movement should give hope to the modern middle-aged woman who harbors needless fears that she is too old and inexperienced to begin participating in the world of the arts, in business, or in public life. And she need not be deterred

—which constitutes a fourth of the population of our country and which receives more than half the nation's total income. This group is at its peak in the economy, in the community, and in political strength.

In 1950 there were 30.8 million people between forty-five and sixty-four; in 1970, 41.8 million. By 1975, the figure is expected to rise to about 43.3 million before it drops slightly to reflect the lower birthrates of the Great Depression and World War II. In the 1968 census, there were 21.2 million women and 19.5 million men from forty-five to sixty-four. Seven-eighths of the men and more than four-fifths of the women were married. There were relatively few middle-aged widowers, but 7.9 per cent of the women in the first decade of middle age were widows. The percentage soared to 22 per cent for women fifty-five to sixty-four. A first marriage in middle age is rare, but more than a fourth of all people who remarry are in that age bracket.

Among the other data that have been gathered on the middle-ager is the fact that he is less likely to move to a new home than is a younger person, a reflection of his stability in society. He has greater social prestige, more money in the bank, and smaller debts; and 41 per cent of all stockholders are middle-aged. Fifteen million women over forty-five, most of them married, hold full-time jobs.

THE POTENTIALS OF WOMEN

A woman knows when she starts the job of bearing and rearing children that her "employment" will run out. If she gives any thought to the matter, she will wisely accept —and even look forward to—the inevitable by preparing for the day when she can hang up her apron and choose a new career, something in which she is really interested that will enable her to expand upon her talents. Whatever she decides, she certainly has had plenty of time to think about it and to act upon her inclinations. A woman who is surprised and discouraged at suddenly landing kerplunk in middle-age idleness has only herself to chastise for her failure to plan ahead.

If the middle-aged woman had nothing to contribute, she might well become a burden not only to herself and her family but to society, but in the next decade this great resource of 40 million women over forty can—and should—be drawn upon for many services. Many more teachers and college instructors will be needed, along with a million health-service specialists, 4.5 million state and local government employees, and countless clerical and secretarial workers. What better source is there than the woman eager to start a new career?

A POSITIVE VIEW OF YOUTH PRESSURES

One of the scores of experts interviewed for this book, Bernice Neugarten, chairman of the Committee on Human Development at the University of Chicago, takes a positive view of the women beset from all sides by youth pressures. Middle-aged—and older—people have always felt some threats from the young, she emphasizes, just as they have always felt great pride in them, "because, after all, it's their investments in the young that they live to see materialize." However, she, like others, notes that the mass media have been publicizing youth in a way that makes it appear, superficially at least, as if the junior citizenry pose a greater threat than ever to the middle-aged; in actual fact, however, this threat may be no different from before—just louder, with the help of television's pervasive commercials catering to juvenile consumers of all ages.

"Some people in middle age may face what they call a

crisis," Dr. Neugarten has observed, "but I don't think crises are ever related to one age period rather than another in the sense that marriage is a crisis for most people, and certainly adjusting to parenthood is a crisis. If you mean by 'crisis' some new role change in the life cycle that calls for all sorts of new adaptations, then in that sense middle age is another one of the crises. But if you mean that it tends to make people mentally ill at a higher frequency rate than at other periods of their lives, then I don't think it should be seen as 'crisis' in that sense. I am impressed with the number of middle-aged people whom I have spoken with, particularly upper-middle-class people, professional men and women, who tend to have a more favorable than unfavorable view of middle age, who feel that they have come into their own and that they know how to manage themselves and their time."

This may be a period in which there is some loss of youth, Dr. Neugarten admits, but many people of mature years are happier than they were when they were groping through their lives, not knowing where they were headed. "The forty- to sixty-year-old range is a distinctive period in life, and in particular for women, because it tends to be a period when most women's responsibilities for child rearing have ended, or at least tapered off to the extent where there isn't very much in the way of demand for the mothering aspect of a woman's life. That makes a very major change, and I also think that women now, compared to men, tend to see this as a time when a new life begins and a whole new freedom begins."

It is obvious, as Dr. Neugarten is willing to accept, that this may be a less clear-cut change for professional women or those who have been achievers than for the wife who has spent most of her time keeping house and looking after children. For the "retired" housewife, the period around forty can be a time for shifting gears, a time in which she establishes a new pace of living and finds new ways to spend time, to reassess her life, and to recognize that she has entered a period that is quite different from the preceding years.

A major stumbling block noted by Dr. Neugarten in connection with middle age is the fact that people tend to dread the unfamiliar. This is true of women who pause to take a look at themselves in mid-life, particularly in the light of the changes produced by menopause or the departure of grown children. Those women often find the experience to be less traumatic than they had feared. The pause that depresses some often refreshes others.

"I think that most middle-aged people would not trade places at all with the young, not for a minute," Dr. Neugarten said. "In that sense they find it more comfortable to be forty or fifty than twenty or twenty-five. Lots of middle-aged women would like to look young, but nobody wants to *be* young, and that's a very major difference. What keeps middle-aged people alive and trying to be young might very well be turned around. We might hope that we would keep young people alive by making them a little more mature."

BEWARE OF THE YOUTH-CULT SICKNESS

Dr. Theodore Isaac Rubin, a well-known New York psychoanalyst and author of *Lisa and David* and the best-selling *The Thin Book by a Formerly Fat Psychiatrist,* has posed the theory that acceptance of age is the key to acceptance of self. He is convinced that the woman who refuses to admit her age, or who lies about it, is giving proof of her self-rejection and, if you will, self-hate. She needs to satisfy a superficial vanity and in doing so falls into the toils of an inescapable cycle in which the more she tries to stay young, the more hopeless she feels and the older she becomes.

"For me," Rubin said, "a pretty, unlined, inexperienced face is fine for a very young girl. On a mature woman, such a face denotes old age and death. On the other hand, a face that shows struggle, experience, growth and change, plus the potential for still more change and development, is a beautiful face, a truly youthful face." Youthful self-growth at any age, he added, requires an emotional investment in other people, in causes, in events, in the real world in which one lives, rather than in the superficial.

Marya Mannes, the writer and critic, is in enthusiastic agreement with Dr. Rubin when she says that she is disquieted by the woman who seems to be thirty-five but is known to be sixty because "a life should leave its traces, and the total lack of them is a negation of experience." Miss Mannes, herself well into her sixties, is one of the most vocal women on the subject of middle age, particularly on the youth-oriented aspect of our society that is found largely in the world of advertising, particularly in magazines and on television. She objects to the Lolita syndrome that has caused the youth-cult sickness in which age is often regarded with contempt. In her view, if you are an interesting woman, you will be as interesting at sixty as you were at thirty—and the same goes for men.

Ilka Chase, the actress, wit, and writer, who admits to being "on the shady side of forty," says that as she looks back over her own life, "it seems to me I really didn't know anything until I got to be about thirty-five. I feel that was sort of a plateau I reached, where I began to have perhaps a little common sense, a modicum of wisdom, a little bit of a sense of proportion." But inexperienced as today's young people may be, she feels that they need to realize that there are points of view other than their own, that "even those old, old creatures over the age of forty years who can barely get around on their sticks and with their false teeth and things, are not total imbeciles just because they are forty and over."

One thing that makes life tough for older women, Miss Chase says, is the fact that widowers and divorced men of any age tend to have eyes only for very young women. As a professional woman, she does not have most of the problems of the average housewife, who is supported by her husband, has children, and keeps house, but at the same time she sees no reason why any woman cannot go out to meet life halfway. "I think that she should maintain a certain independence all through her life. There is no reason to be bored—really there is not."

SOME HISTORICAL PERSPECTIVES

Dr. Paul Popenoe, founder and head of the American Institute of Family Relations in Los Angeles, emphasized in a paper on problems after forty that the concerns of middle age are based on the same fears and insecurities we have carried from childhood. We have also developed a habit of measuring life in decades, with no birthdays "as thrilling or as threatening as those with a zero attached to them. Ten, twenty, thirty are stepping-stones toward adult independence; forty, fifty, sixty are millstones around the neck of middle age; seventy, eighty, ninety are milestones on the road of triumphant old age. In the twenties we acquire a family; in the thirties we acquire things; in the forties we acquire anxieties. Suddenly life is half spent in spite of the scientifically increased life-span. It is a moment for reckoning with both the past and the future, a time for self-evaluation and for the reevaluation of accomplishments and goals. The way in which we live in our forties determines our attitudes toward the fifties and sixties, and whether or not we live to enjoy the seventies, eighties and nineties."

A ray of hope may be found in, of all places, the cigarette commercial that sings out, "You've come a long way, baby," which might have been written specifically for middle-aged American women. Just think a minute about the strides that have been made in enabling women not only to live longer but to live better. The life expectancy of an American girl born in the seventeenth century was about eighteen years, and those eighteen years were difficult. At the time of the Civil War, the life expectancy had risen to about forty; in 1900, it was nearly fifty, and by 1970, it had jumped to between seventy-three and eighty. Longevity is the result of advances in nutrition, hygiene, sanitation, and medicine, particularly during childbearing years, and other improvements in living standards. Being a woman a century ago meant being a lifetime manual laborer, a plight from which women have been released by gadgetry, instant foods, and all sorts of labor-saving devices. There have been other advances too. For example, we have come to take for granted the low mortality rate in childbirth, but a visit to any colonial cemetery will tell the story of many young women who died bearing children. The gravestone of many a head of a family is found in the midst of the graves of one, two, or three wives, each of whom died at an age that would indicate they did not survive childbirth. And with them are buried infants and young children.

Anne Simon, author of *The New Years and the New Middle Age*, points out that our grandmothers—and even our mothers—had no function in society by the time they were fifty unless they happened to be unusual people—which many of them were. Now, however, she notes, when a woman is forty or fifty she has in a sense entered her independent, mature, and productive era. "This is the time she can have a marvelous marriage without children to worry about—without that kind of household responsibility—a wonderful and exciting job. And she knows what she wants to do, which is something that cannot be known until you've lived twenty or thirty years of adult life."

At the turn of the century, by the time children had grown up and left home, one of the parents—usually the father—had died, and few widows remarried in those days. Middle age is easier today because of the increased chances that husbands will live through this period. One break women get is that they do not have to make as radical a change in their lives as do the men faced with retirement from their jobs. Women lose their fertility, which the majority of men retain most of their lives, but this certainly should be looked upon as a boon, particularly in a family that has grown children and grandchildren. To Mrs. Simon, the most important thing at any age is to keep changing. "If we don't keep changing and responding to the kind of situations we find ourselves in, we then go to seed and go to sleep mentally, emotionally and in every other way. But if you can find in each new situation that life brings to you—and they certainly are new—a kind of excitement and explorer's enthusiasm, then you can be sure that discovering this new middle age can be as exciting an adventure as any that you come across in your life."

Not only are more people surviving into and through middle age, but it is a period that lasts longer than before. In past generations, middle age was considered to last about fifteen years. Now it has about doubled, creating what Barbara Fried calls a transitional generation. In her book *The Middle Age Crisis,* Mrs. Fried points out that this is the first middle generation to have gone through most of its life enjoying the benefits of miracle drugs, improved nutrition, and easier working conditions. It is also the first to become aware of the need for acceptance and encouragement of and accommodation to the new, vigorous middle-agers that science has turned loose on society.

These are, in truth, the *new* middle years, and they call for the end of the disrespect for age reflected by some of the phony values of the youth cult. Mrs. Fried has said that until we stop overestimating the desirability of youth, we cannot develop a healthy attitude toward middle age. While it is all right to appreciate young people, she says, those in middle age have a right to demand equal time for maturity or risk the prospect of finishing their lives feeling like second-class citizens.

Mrs. Fried reassures women by telling them that the most wonderful thing about middle age is that it gives them a chance to start over again with new wisdom and compassion, to borrow the words of Letitia ("Tish") Baldridge Hollensteiner, who was Mrs. John F. Kennedy's White House press secretary. Mrs. Hollensteiner finds that a little grace can add considerable zest to one's appreciation of the little things in life. "A middle-aged person's attractiveness to others perhaps entails his giving a little more than he did in his youth," she says. "He has to read a little more, observe a little more acutely. If he does all this, how can he help but be nicer to have around than when he was young?"

In the discussion on Aline Saarinen's program mentioned earlier, Mrs. Fried expressed the view that every woman has to approach adjustment to middle age in her own way. The woman who has worked all her life can continue to do so without feeling guilty about it or encountering conflicts. The woman who finds she has to change her life pattern sharply is, in Mrs. Fried's view, faced with certain conflicts not necessarily dependent on whether she works or not, "but it is a fact that you have to make a change at middle age, which is really the crux of the problem."

As has been pointed out, women in middle age can be attractive, physically and sexually. The late Dr. Anna K. Daniels, gynecologist and marriage counselor, described as completely false the notion that a woman *must* lose her beauty and allure simply because she has passed menopause. With proper medical care and restoration of glandular balance through the hormone treatments a doctor prescribes, "there is no reason today for any woman to wither like an old apple." As for sex, Dr. William H. Masters and Virginia E. Johnson, the research scientists who have conducted extensive studies of sexuality, find that "many a woman develops renewed interest in her husband and in the physical maintenance of her own person, and has described a 'second honeymoon' during her early fifties. This expression of unleashed sexual drive occasioned by the alleviation of the 'pregnancy phobia' is one of the most frequently occurring factors responsible for increased sexual tensions evident in the fifty to sixty age group."

Phyllis Diller, the comedienne, has developed her own philosophy for middle age; it is one that others might want to apply to their daily lives. She says: "Every morning brings an opportunity. Each day is all yours. You can do anything you want with it within your framework of responsibility. If you are a housewife, you can be nice to the kids and the neighbors and not yell at the milkman and the butcher. If you are a star, you can spread a little cheer by smiling at the people who work with you and serve you."

It is to help other women not only to take advantage of the opportunities offered by each new day but to create some opportunities of their own that this book has been written, and we offer as the first possibility for creating a fresh approach to life the years of the menopause, which too many women regard as an ending, whereas in actuality it can become a bright beginning.

CHAPTER
2

No Need to Sing the Menopause Blues

"DO YOU THINK it is getting a little warm in here, or is it just me?"

Those are the passwords to middle age for many women, and they are a giveaway to the fact that menopause has set in, for they signal the onset of what are known as hot flushes or flashes. When a woman starts complaining of the heat in December or fans herself with her program in an air-conditioned theater, she may be letting the world in on the fact that her menstrual cycle is spinning slowly to a halt and her years of fertility are drawing to an end.

For obvious reasons, women in the throes of the off-and-on-again blanket syndrome tend to be secretive about the onset of the menopause, also known as the climacteric, despite the fact that every young girl knows from the time she first menstruates that some day the process will stop if she lives long enough. She is aware that "the change of life" or simply "the change" is bound to come and will mean that she is inching into old age. Her awareness that there is a tendency to thicken at the waistline, develop a few wrinkles and sags, and start turning gray at about this time fills her years with mounting apprehension until the day she first misses a menstrual period and the first hot flash envelops her with a disconcerting glow.

Women tend to approach middle age with clenched fists largely because of their dread of the menopause and what it means in their lives, in the opinion of Dr. Sherwin Kaufman, a New York gynecologist. Although menopause usually begins at about age fifty, women are already beginning to think about and even to anticipate what is to come when they turn forty. Why do we say "anticipate"? Because many women look forward eagerly to the time when they can enjoy sexual freedom without fear of pregnancy. "There are many things a woman can fear as she gets older," Dr. Kaufamn says, "but menopause needn't be faced with fear and trepidation; with understanding, it can be faced with relative calm."

The adage that ignorance is bliss does not hold true in this instance, for much of the concern stems from a lack of understanding of the biological bridge between youth and old age. Some years ago Bernice Neugarten initiated a series of studies at the University of Chicago on the attitudes of middle-class women toward the change of life. She found they tended to shy away from the subject in exchanging confidences, as if somehow "the whole menopause was a kind of taboo topic." Dr. Neugarten noted that her subjects were eager for information and, to her surprise, she discovered that the younger ones tended to be the most apprehensive. Both young and old confessed that they did not know whether anything could be done about "the change." "Doctors won't talk to us about it," some said, while others complained that they were unable to find anything to read to prepare them for what was to come.

Actually, books, pamphlets, and articles on the subject abound, and it is doubtful that any gynecologist or family physician would refuse to discuss the menopause with any woman who was sincere in seeking advice. Women's organizations and other groups sponsor discussions and symposiums dealing with the topic, and there are a number of good films offering constructive guidance.

Yet even in our enlightened age, many women still give credence to old wives' tales about menopause, while at the same time pooh-poohing them. They readily recite the "dangers" of menopause: depression, mental breakdown, loss of sex appeal, creeping senility. They project their own anxieties with comments such as "*I* don't have any problems, but I know women who have gone through real crises with the menopause."

Release from stereotyped conceptions—and misconceptions—can be achieved through education in the basics of human biology. That there has been some progress in this area through the years is reassuring; we no longer expect a woman to wither and die because her ovaries have dried up, a fate that apparently was widely anticipated in the day of our great-great-grandmothers, as one of the standard volumes of home remedies of the mid-1850s relates. A rather grim picture of middle age was drawn by A. W. Chase, M.D., in his best-selling third "receipt book" entitled *Dr. Chase's Last Receipt Book and Household Physician.* A section headed "Cessation of Menses, or turn of life," paints this startling picture of menopause in a chapter on female "diseases":

"That period of life at which the menses cease to flow is likewise very critical to the sex. The stoppage of any customary evacuation, however small, is sufficient to *disorder the whole frame, and often to destroy life itself* [italics ours]. Hence, it comes to pass, that so many women either fall into chronic disorders, or die about this time; such of them, however, as survive it, without contracting any chronic disease, often become more healthy and hardy than they were before, and enjoy strength and vigor to a very great age."

Dr. Chase went on to advise that if menstruation ceases suddenly in women "of a full habit," they "ought to abate somewhat of their usual quantity of food, especially of the more nourishing kind, as flesh, eggs, etc. They ought likewise to take sufficient exercise, and, to keep the bowels open. This may be done by taking, once or twice a week, a little rhubarb, or an infusion of hiera picra in wine or brandy, or purgatives. . . . and if complicated with other diseases, call a doctor."

ORIGINS OF SOME MYTHS

How did distorted notions arise about such an important milestone in the life cycle? They certainly were not handed down from the days of antiquity, when few women lived beyond their reproductive years and many were old before their time in societies that provided no medical care during childbirth and in which women toiled long and hard. As far as Dr. Margaret Mead, the anthropologist, has been able to determine, there are no ceremonies in still-primitive societies that mark the onset of menopause commensurate with rites celebrating the advent of fertility signaled by menstruation. The few women in those societies who live beyond the menopause are treated in much the same way as men, and most of the taboos that inhibited them during their reproductive years are dropped. No one frowns when one of those "old" women makes an obscene joke or enters into the kind of camaraderie with men that was forbidden her as a younger woman. She is also less restricted in her activities than she was when her life revolved around bearing and caring for children.

In the earliest times, a number of societies isolated women during their menstrual periods. The Jews of biblical days—and, indeed, some of the more extremely conservative Jewish groups today—placed the menstruating woman in purdah. She was not allowed to enter the temple during this time and, when possible, was confined to a special tent. The Book of Leviticus sets forth strictures against having intercourse during menstruation, providing for penalties ranging from exile or death for the woman to seven days of isolation for the man in which to become ritually purified.

Menopause is at the heart of one of the major stories in the Book of Genesis. Dr. Robert B. Greenblatt, an endocrinologist and professor at the Medical College of Georgia, in a special study of the Bible from a physician's point of view, found the story of Abraham and Sarah to be that of an aging man and a menopausal woman. The key passage cited by Dr. Greenblatt was: "Now Abraham and Sarah were old and well-stricken in age; and it ceased to be with Sarah after the manner of women." Dr. Greenblatt diagnosed her "cantankerous and irritable" behavior as that of a woman going through the climacteric. He theorized that she probably often upbraided Abraham because life had "passed her by"; having borne no children, she was left without proof of her womanhood. Sarah accused Abraham of being sterile and challenged him to "go unto my maid" to prove it. Abraham did as his wife requested and "went in unto Hagar, and she conceived."

This elementary test of male fertility so hurt and angered Sarah that she ordered Hagar from the house. "It was then," Greenblatt recounted, "that the Lord mercifully opened Sarah's womb; she bore a son and his name was Isaac." The birth, mentioned several times in the Old Testament, indicates that Sarah resumed ovulation long enough to conceive what is called today "a change-of-life baby."

WHAT EXACTLY IS THE CLIMACTERIC IN WOMEN

While most women know at least *some* of the facts of their biological lives and many are aware of most of them, a surprising number have little knowledge about the inner workings of their bodies. At the risk of providing too much information—or information that may seem too elementary for some—we feel that a step-by-step account of the menopause and the stages leading up to it may be helpful.

The word *climacteric* is Greek in origin, with roots in a term meaning "rung of the ladder." It is often used interchangeably with the term *menopause,* although there is a distinction. In a literal sense, the rungs of a ladder represent definite changes in the sequence of life, with the menopausal climacteric denoting a gradual slackening and ultimate cessation of menstruation, along with other related changes in the body. This process usually takes place over several years.

Menopause is also Greek in origin, drawn from two words denoting "month" and "cessation." The cessation of the monthly menses, marking the end of the reproductive cycle, is the most easily identifiable sign of the climacteric.

In nearly all other animals the female reproductive cycle is closely related to the length of life itself, and the female usually dies soon after the ovaries cease to function. In the human animal, however, the female far outlives her reproductive capacity, with the menopause a transitional period. With increasing longevity, menopause occurs more nearly toward the midpoint of the American woman's life.

THE FACTS OF MENOPAUSE

For a full understanding of menopause, one needs to know something about the menstrual cycle and the functions of the sex organs and endocrine glands. Girls and boys grow at about the same rate until the age of seven or eight, when girls begin to shoot ahead. At this time, a girl's ovaries, which have been fully formed since birth, begin sending out minute but ever-increasing amounts of the female hormone estrogen. Produced through natural stimulation from the pituitary gland at the base of the brain, estrogen figures significantly in the development of secondary sex characteristics such as the widening of the pelvis, the budding of the breasts, and the growth of female-patterned hair. They include also the smooth skin texture associated with femininity, hair that is usually more luxuriant than that of the male, and the maturity of reproductive organs. Because of estrogen's role in body and bone development, it contributes to general growth.

During puberty—between the ages of eleven and fourteen, as a rule—the pituitary gland begins to secrete other hormones, gonadotrophins, which stimulate the ovaries to produce and release eggs every month. This brings about a dramatic change in a girl's life—the rung on the ladder known as menstruation—which is the basis of a woman's fertility. Monthly periods of menstruation, marking the end of one cycle of ovulation and the beginning of the next, occur when the lining of the womb, or uterus, is shed. And each month the flow of estrogen and another hormone, progesterone, prepares the lining of the uterus —the endometrium—for possible pregnancy. If an egg is not fertilized, so that conception does not occur, the mucous lining of the uterus drops off in the form of menstrual flow.

Essentially, the menstrual cycle is an intricate twenty-eight-day pattern of hormonal rise and fall. The length of the cycle varies, as does the duration of menstrual flow, with the normal discharge lasting from three to seven days. At the end of the period, during which hormonal levels have dropped, the supply of estrogen generated by the pituitary begins to rise again to stimulate the ovaries and start another monthly cycle.

This rhythmical series of changes in the sex organs occurs throughout a woman's reproductive life, interrupted only by pregnancy or perhaps an occasional unusual condition such as a sudden change in climate or altitude or an emotional or physical problem. When pregnancy occurs, the manufacture of estrogen and progesterone soars to many times their usual levels. A woman whose system follows a normal cycle produces a minute amount of estrogen, while during the latter weeks of pregnancy, she may generate large quantities. Such a flooding of the body with hormones makes a woman truly bloom.

Some thirty to forty years after the onset of menstruation, depending on the individual, a woman's childbearing years end, putting her on the rung of the ladder known as menopause. Menstrual cycles become shorter or longer and irregular and finally cease. Sometimes the change comes overnight; sometimes it is a gradual tapering-off process lasting a few months or perhaps years.

THE PHYSIOLOGY OF MENOPAUSE

With the slackening of the output of estrogen and progesterone, physiological changes occur, depending in extent and intensity on physical and emotional stamina and on personality. Poor health can bring about a difficult menopause, and an inability to cope with life's crises may compound the situation. Regardless of the severity, diminished production of estrogen obviously affects the "target organs," the breasts and genitals, which have been the major recipients of the sex hormones stimulated by the pituitary gland and transmitted through the body.

Every woman knows that in old age the breasts tend to sag and shrink. Why? Because the shutting off of hormonal flow diminishes the glandular tissue and tone of the breasts, causing the ligaments to relax. Sagging is an inevitable result. Along with this comes a gradual thinning and atrophy of the lining of the uterus. The cervical canal leading to the uterus narrows and the lining of the vagina gradually loses its elasticity and becomes thin. A similar reduction in the urethra and part of the bladder may occur.

Such changes occur over a period of years, usually in direct ratio to the decline of estrogen production. They affect the autonomic nervous system, which links the nerves, organs, and muscles, possibly causing a variety of psychosomatic complaints and definitely bringing about specific physical signs, the most classic of which is the hot flash. There is no more common or troublesome symptom of menopause than the flash, which is a periodic dilation of the small blood vessels of the skin. Sudden onsets of what feels like a fever, often accompanied by sweat and patches of redness, usually begin at the chest and sweep upward over the throat and face. Drs. Robert H. Glass and Nathan G. Kase of Yale University find in their book *Woman's Choice* that flashes are dramatically related to hormonal deprivation as evidenced in the rapidity with which they are eliminated by administration of modest doses of estrogen.

Although some women slide easily through menopause, encountering nothing more than menstrual irregularity, others develop a variety of distressing physical symptoms in addition to hot flashes. These may be related to autonomic phenomena such as a sensation that the heart is occasionally racing or pounding (tachycardia) or that the pulse seems to be unusually rapid. There may be a sensation of numbness in the hands and feet (paresthesia) or a crawling or tingling feeling on the skin (formication). Less well defined physical symptoms include insomnia, headaches, dizziness, arthralgia (pain and swelling in the joints), and gastrointestinal disturbances, including constipation or diarrhea, loss of appetite, and vague abdominal pains.

In seeking to determine how many physical complaints are reported during menopause, Dr. Kaufman reviewed the histories of two hundred women who had been under his care. He counted fifty symptoms. Not all women who have complaints take them to doctors, however; many suffer alone and muddle through—perhaps making themselves and everyone around them miserable without knowing that help is available. Several surveys indicate that anywhere from a mere 10 to 30 per cent actually seek help (Dr. Kaufman thinks the figure may be closer to 50 per cent) because women, like many physicians, tend to show more concern for the health of others than for their own well-being. A mother learns to be a devoted nurse for her children. As a wife she is constantly alert to her husband's aches and pains. But what does she do for herself? Does she have a checkup as regularly as her husband and children do? Does she visit her gynecologist as often as she sees her dentist? The answer in most cases, as Dr. Kaufman indicates, is probably no, so that when she approaches middle age and begins to feel the early symptoms of some of the physical problems that can occur with advancing years, she may react by rushing off to the doctor in a panic, fearing that she is suddenly "falling apart," or she may ignore the problem as best she can and simply accept it as one of the facts of later life. Either way she is suffering for her self-neglect.

Because in the past women over forty have often been regarded as neurotic or hypochondriacal, a woman today may steer clear of regular visits to her doctor lest she be accused of suffering from "imaginitis." Well, no one has to be sick to make an appointment with a physician, particularly in a day of preventive medicine, and there is no need to overwork the word *psychosomatic* just because one cares enough about herself to have a periodic checkup.

Some women avoid medical examinations out of fear. They dread that the doctor might detect a telltale lump on the breast or irregularities in the cell structure of the uterus. Vanity may keep a woman from the possibility that she might need a hearing aid or eyeglasses. She may require special attention for her teeth and gums, which develop new vulnerabilities in middle age, or may be plagued by varicose veins. Unfortunately, most of us tend at times to hide from the truth and hide the truth from ourselves instead of being realistic and declaring that it is time to "join the club."

There really is no reason why many kinds of sickness or even some of the aches and pains women encounter *must* be part of getting older. While women seem to incur more ailments and disabilities than men—nearly all associated with the fact that they are female—they are not likely to die from them. No one has ever heard of the menopause killing anyone.

EMOTIONAL FACTORS IN THE CHANGING YEARS

The menopause can cause emotional distress, for just as a hormonal imbalance may create endocrine disorientation, so it may bring about emotional disorientation, as during puberty, when the adolescent girl sometimes manifests sharp changes in mood, ranging from mild upsets to severe depression and perhaps even hysteria.

Until relatively recent years, reproduction was regarded as a woman's primary function. It was natural for her to have negative thoughts about menopause, for it not only made her feel as though she was losing her womanhood and attraction, but it also filled her with dread of old age and its infirmities. Menopause therefore meant to many the loss of their raison d'être. Here is where a little understanding on the part of husbands can go a long way. Perhaps understandably, many women are reluctant to discuss their flashes and other menopausal symptoms with their husbands, and husbands, in their turn, are likely to become impatient with women who go through periods of nervousness or depression or complain that it is either too hot or too cold. Open discussion of the menopause and its problems can help, and it would not be asking too much for men unable to grasp their wives' mental, emotional, and physical situations to have a talk with the family doctor about what is happening and why and how the family can help.

Fortunately, attitudes have changed with increased understanding of the potential of a woman's mature years and with the medical advances that have eliminated much of the stress and distress of the change of life. Still, some women persist in passing through periods of sadness and purposelessness at menopause, while others withdraw into themselves, tending to exaggerate minor difficulties and illnesses and even going so far as to develop extreme, incapacitating psychosomatic illnesses. Anxiety, irritability, and depression are often compounded by headaches and palpitations. Pains throb in the temples or at the back of the neck, while palpitations tighten the chest until their victim feels as though she is about to burst. In their anguish some women conjure up the myths they have heard all their lives and become terrified at the thought that they may be suffering from heart trouble or be on the verge of a breakdown.

Panic over such worries is unwarranted, for, as Dr. Edward Steiglitz has noted, "a woman has less chance of going out of her mind during the menopause than she has of having a brick fall off a roof and fracture her skull on the way home from a shopping tour." Only about six women in every hundred thousand are known to have suffered from an "involutional psychosis," the technical term for the regression—or process of mental decline or decay—that can occur after middle life.

While severe mental illness is not a serious threat, the emotional instability a woman may suffer in menopause can cause much distress. When a woman is so afflicted, she is not the only one involved, for her emotional problems can upset an entire family. "If not overcome," says Dr. G. Lombard Kelly, "they can cause lasting harm to a woman's personality. While deep psychological problems often require specialized assistance, many doctors find a restoration of hormonal balance helps promote a sense of physical and emotional peace."

TREATMENT CAN HELP

Until only a few decades ago the menopause was considered to be such a natural part of the aging process that its attendant discomforts simply had to be accepted. That is no longer true, in the view of an increasing number of gynecologists who have challenged antiquated concepts. "Menopause is a physiological phenomenon and not a disease process," according to Drs. Glass and Kase. "However, the deleterious consequences of estrogen deprivation are of such significance to the individual that these demand treatment. Happily, this is available. While some hesitation exists in conservative medical circles, an increasing number of physicians believe that replacement with estrogen is beneficial. In this view, all women should receive hormone therapy after menopause."

Long before a woman stops menstruating, her ovaries gradually become less active; hormone production tapers off, although it may still continue after menopause. There is evidence that some estrogen is also produced by the adrenal glands, which provide an important source of the hormone after menopause. However, replacing the missing estrogen with carefully controlled medication has become common practice. This is something only a doctor can decide; there must be a determination of whether hormones are necessary, in what dosage, and for how long. In his book on *The Ageless Woman,* Dr. Kaufman observed that no therapy is needed if a woman has no complaints and no apparent deficiency of hormones. However, he added, if symptoms appear suggesting estrogen imbalance and there are no medical reasons to rule out therapy, he usually gives what he calls a "therapeutic test" with estrogen. He tells a patient that if her symptoms are due to a shortage of estrogen, relief may be expected. But hormones cannot relieve problems resulting from other causes.

Once therapy is begun, a woman is advised to see her physician every six months so that she can be observed closely. Regular checkups facilitate a continuing reassessment of estrogen activity and lead to any necessary changes in the treatment plan. The therapy really is no more radical than that provided the millions of people who take daily thyroid tablets. The body does not care whether its vital substances, such as thyroid or hormones, are produced internally or introduced externally. Hormone therapy, then, does not mean the introduction of an element that was not in the body before; it is simply replacing an ingredient that the body is no longer able to generate for itself.

Dr. Glass pointed out in an interview that with women now living far past the menopause, they often manage to thrive for at least a third of their lives in an estrogen-deprived state. "Now while this is so-called natural deprivation," he said, "there's no reason not to alleviate it. We do so with other things we consider natural. Childbirth is a natural process, and yet we do it in the hospital and use medication to help the woman. There is no reason not to replace this loss of estrogen.

"We have to realize that hormones are not a panacea," he added. "We're not saying that. We're saying that there is no reason for the woman to have estrogen deprivation or whatever other problems she is having in the menopause. The estrogen will not keep her feminine forever. There is an aging process that goes on independent of hormones. But we're saying that a lot of rough spots in menopause can be smoothed out by use of continuous estrogen medication."

EARLY AND ARTIFICIAL MENOPAUSE

There are cases in which menstruation ceases as early as the twenties or thirties. Such premature menopause need not be analagous to the menopause of middle age, for it is sometimes possible to reverse the situation and restore ovulation with estrogen replacement or other therapy. The first task of the physician is to try to determine why the situation has arisen; what he decides to do about it comes later. Dr. Kaufman feels that estrogen replacement is of particular importance for such younger women not only to prevent premature atrophy but because infertility may not yet be irreversible. On the other hand, nothing can be done to rejuvenate the ovaries of older women. Medical measures that may restore ovulation to the younger woman may also restore normal menstruation; not so with the woman in middle age.

There are rare cases in which women go through an early, permanent menopause in their mid-thirties; there may be family histories of early menopause, which suggests that heredity has something to do with it. Early menopause can be treated successfully with the administration of hormones in the form of the now-familiar pills available on prescription. Dr. Elizabeth Connell, associate professor of obstetrics and gynecology at Columbia Presbyterian Medical Center in New York, has words of reassurance on this score: "Any woman who has gone through an early menopause faces many years without estrogens and I think we all, as doctors, know the effects on skin, on bone. There are effects on mental attitude, on many things. And women who show the effects of the loss of estrogen can be very effectively treated."

Artificial menopause—induced at early ages, usually by surgery—creates other problems. Treatment is based on the type of surgery, which becomes necessary when ovaries, uterus, or tubes are diseased. A total hysterectomy—removal of the uterus, including the cervix, but *not* the ovaries and their tubes—would not of itself necessitate the administration of replacement hormones since it is the ovaries that secrete them. A panhysterectomy—removal of the entire uterus, tubes, *and* ovaries—would call for immediate therapy, possibly beginning in the hospital, for although the adrenal glands supply some estrogen, they cannot produce nearly enough to spare a woman from going into a sudden decline.

ESTROGEN AND CANCER

Just about everyone—particularly women—has become cancer conscious, thanks to effective campaigns in the press and broadcasting media and the insistence of many doctors on regular examinations. Some misconceptions that hormones are a potential cause of cancer persist, however, which builds up resistance and anxiety among menopausal women who might otherwise be helped through replacement therapy.

What are the facts? Dr. Robert A. Wilson of Brooklyn Methodist Hospital, head of the Wilson Research Foundation, has pointed out that the incidence of cancer is low among women during their young and fertile years when natural estrogen levels are high, while the number of cases rises in later life as the levels fall. To this observation, Dr. Kaufman adds that more than 90 per cent of uterine cancers occur in women over forty, when their stores of estrogen are waning. The incidence of breast cancer also increases with age, he notes.

Dr. Glass and Dr. Kase maintain that no tumor in a human has been blamed on estrogen. "Reports of tumor induction in animals involved strains which ordinarily run a high risk of spontaneous cancer," they said. "Furthermore, the doses of estrogen used were many times stronger than those required for human application. To be sure, there are human cancers, notably of the breast and uterine endometrium, which may be stimulated but not caused by estrogen. Obviously, women with these tumors or those having been cured of them should not risk further stimulation which might accompany replacement therapy." In other words, some women cannot take estrogens, in which case physicians often prescribe tranquilizers to help them over rough periods.

The major element of prevention involved in estrogen therapy is that women in such programs make a point of visiting their gynecologists twice a year for checkups, which include a pelvic examination and a Pap smear. The latter procedure, named after the late Dr. George N. Papanicolaou, is a simple, easy, and quick cancer-screening procedure, which probably has saved more lives and prevented more misery among women than any medical advance except perhaps the measures that have made childbirth safer and more painless. The physician removes a small amount of the vaginal secretion from the cervical area with a cotton-tipped applicator and a wooden tongue depressor. This substance is applied to a glass slide and examined under a microscope for the presence of cancer cells. The same smear can be used to take an estrogen count, which helps to determine whether therapy is warranted.

Early in 1972 an announcement was made of another potential major breakthrough with the development of a device for taking uterine cell smears that may eventually provide early warning of developing cancer of the uterus. If this procedure proves to be as successful as its creators hope, it may be an even greater lifesaver than the Pap test.

Some women—and some doctors, too—have resisted hormone treatment for women in menopause; other doctors tell their patients that as soon as they feel their first hot flash, or whenever the flashes become bothersome, relief is available. And relief does come almost as soon as the pill-taking regimen (three weeks on the pill and one week off is the usual prescription) is begun. One of those who believes that the use of estrogen therapy is spreading is Dr. Joseph Goldzieher, director of the Division of Clinical Sciences at the Southwest Foundation for Research and Education in San Antonio, Texas.

"I think," he observes, "there has already been a revolution in the attitude of my colleagues over the past five to ten years. They have been worried about cancer, and quite justifiably. The cancer has not appeared. The vital statistics over the past thirty years show absolutely no increase in breast cancer in the population of women who would now be showing it if, indeed, these worrisome predictions had been true."

WHAT "THEY" THINK ABOUT MENOPAUSE

Despite the openness that has developed in our society in discussions of sex, the introduction of the subject of menopause at a dinner party would almost certainly put a dead hand on the conversation. Apparently it repels some people, mainly women who have not yet encountered it and men who somehow have come to regard it as a symbol of antisex. It is almost a certainty that if a woman, however attractive, were to suddenly blurt, "Here comes a hot flash!" while sipping a Martini at a cocktail party, she would "turn off" any man of any age who happened to be chatting with her. Mentioning such an occurrence would be as out of place as announcing that "I have my period," but the reaction to the latter would be far less dramatic because there is a stigma—and an understandable one—attached to the menopause.

Yes, society does look upon women of middle age with a degree of suspicion because of the fact of life that is menopause. It is a suspicion that has been carried to ridiculous extremes. There are those who are convinced that menopause automatically brings on irrational and difficult behavior. Probably the most outrageous example of this was the declaration by Dr. Eugene Berman, a Maryland surgeon and member of the Democratic Party's Committee on National Priority, who is on record as saying that women make poor executives because of their "raging hormones." In a discussion on whether a woman would qualify for the Presidency of the United States, he expressed apprehension that a menopausal woman who had to act in a Bay of Pigs crisis might act irrationally and emotionally and plunge the nation into a crisis. He neglected to state that men go through a certain amount of emotionalism on occasion when they reach the same age

—the male climacteric is a well-established clinical phenomenon—and the cries of protest against his remarks served to emphasize how old-fashioned and prejudiced such views are. (The protests triggered his retirement from the committee.)

That some men go through a kind of "menopausal" depression during their fifties, when many of their early dreams and ambitions have come to naught, was emphasized by Dr. Esther Ann Grayzel, an endocrinologist and assistant professor of medicine at the Albert Einstein College of Medicine. "It is not known whether these problems in men are hormonal in origin," she said, "but there certainly are in this period depression and even suicide attempts and many psychosomatic problems, so I don't think it's a unisex situation. I think there are problems in either sex. Contrary to Dr. Berman's comments, sometimes there's a positive effect from the female hormones, and this has been noted through many years."

There are those who are convinced that the aging female is more stable than the man in his middle years. One of these is Dr. Michael Baden, deputy chief medical examiner of New York City, who has observed that women executives are much less likely to commit suicide than are their male counterparts. Moreover, he said, the major disease of middle life, hardening of the arteries—arteriosclerosis, especially as it involves the blood vessels of the heart, causing heart attacks, and the blood vessels of the brain, causing strokes—is much more severe in men than in women. He concluded that a woman executive might be on the job for ten or fifteen years longer than a man with the same training.

Despite their physical stamina, women, like men, need to be aware of some of the physical problems that can accompany middle age. Our teeth need special care, particularly to prevent the onset of gum diseases. We should see our eye specialist annually for precautionary examinations for the early detection of glaucoma and also for any changes needed in our eyeglasses. It is important to undergo regular gynecological examinations—some doctors like to see their women patients twice a year—and we certainly should seek an annual general physical examination that includes an electrocardiogram, a blood sugar test for diabetes, a chest X ray, and a metabolism test.

This leads us back to Bernice Neugarten, the University of Chicago human-development expert, and her survey of women. That survey, in turn, caused her to decide that more public attention and information were needed on the biological changes in middle age among men and women alike. "It strikes me," she said, "that most people today know a great deal more, in general, about good health practices than they did twenty years ago. But I think it is advantageous to make more information available about changes that occur in middle age, and in particular the biology of the female, since these changes, by and large, are more dramatic than those in the male."

She also pointed out that as women grow older and look back upon middle age, they must admit that it did not produce the problems they had anticipated. If more women knew this and had the necessary foreknowledge, they might be better equipped to approach and endure menopause not only with unclenched fists but with an anticipation of happier days ahead.

CHAPTER 3

What Every Young Woman Over Forty Should Know About Sex

LAUGHTER GREETED Cornelia Otis Skinner, the actress and author, on her return home from a confidential interview with Dr. Alfred C. Kinsey when he was collecting the sex secrets of American women. Her husband and son were convulsed at the thought that Miss Skinner, in her dignified middle age, had been deemed an appropriate subject for interrogation about her sex life. Whatever in the world, they demanded to know, could *she* possibly have to tell Dr. Kinsey that would be of scientific interest?

Her indignation at being rebuffed by her family may reflect a typical attitude toward the middle-aged woman when it comes to matters of sex. Somehow it becomes difficult for young people to believe that a mother or, heaven forbid, a grandmother could possibly enjoy the marriage bed, despite abundant recent evidence to counteract the myth that women's interest in sex—and satisfaction from it—wane during and after menopause. Perhaps using Miss Skinner as one of his statistics, the late Dr. Kinsey and his team of investigators reported in their famous study, *Sexual Behavior in the Human Female,* that the facts are quite the contrary. Women, Kinsey and his colleagues observed, tend to become *less* inhibited and *more* interested in sex as they move through the forties and into the fifties—and even on to the sixties.

In another notable study, Dr. William H. Masters and Virginia E. Johnson of the Reproductive Biology Research Foundation in St. Louis found "significant sexual capacity and effective sexual performance" among sixty-one menopausal and postmenopausal women forty to seventy-eight years old. Their controversial report on an eleven-year scientific inquiry into the physiology of sex among nearly eight hundred men and women added a qualifying note, however: Both the intensity of the physiological response and the rapidity of reaction to sexual stimulation tend to lessen with advancing years. They reported, moreover, in *Human Sexual Response* that other reactions appeared to be less pronounced in the older woman: the sexual flush that envelops a woman at orgasm was less predominant; the vagina tended to be dry, with a diminution of natural lubrication; the clitoris was slower to react to direct stimulation; and the orgasm was of shorter duration. Rather than responding negatively, however, Masters and Johnson offered hope for the older woman with the conclusion that "the aging human female is fully capable of sexual performance at orgasmic response levels, particularly if she is exposed to regularity of effective sexual stimulation. . . . There seem to be no physiologic reasons why the frequency of sexual expression found satisfactory for the younger woman should not be carried over into the postmenopausal years. . . . In short, there is no time limit drawn by advancing years to female sexuality."

The Masters and Johnson and the Kinsey studies were in agreement in finding no complaints about the absence of sexual satisfaction among women beyond the age of menopause. Rather, many said they had gained because they were no longer inhibited by the worry about pregnancy. True, the loss of estrogen may have caused some distress, such as vaginal dryness and itching, but hormone replacement today can usually alleviate such problems.

Another boon to the middle-aged woman is the fact that she is likely to have completed the job of child rearing and, once released from the physical, mental, and emotional demands of motherhood, she may be filled with vim and vigor and raring to go. In seeking new outlets for her energy, her interest in sexual activity may be heightened. That is what people are talking about when they refer to the "second honeymoon" phase of middle age. A continued—or revived—interest in sex can be maintained even into the eighties, according to Masters and Johnson in their recent study, *Human Sexual Inadequacy.* Some adjustments to the natural physiological changes that occur with advancing age may be necessary, but Masters and Johnson linked such inadequacy among the aged, particularly women, to the *fear* of a poor "performance." Mrs. Johnson—who subsequently became Mrs. Masters—added that she had a "real thing" about the fact that 95 per cent of what had been written about female sexuality had come from men who had never thought of asking women about their feelings and responses.

One of the important findings by Masters and Johnson was that people who maintain regular sex lives tend to keep some of the attributes of youth. This was borne out in an analysis of the St. Louis studies by the writers Jhan and June Robbins, who reported that a number of the mature couples treated in the Masters and Johnson clinic had just about given up hope of ever resuming an adequate sex life. Before receiving therapy, they assumed that nothing could be done about their inadequacies; some were even on the verge of divorce.

After their sessions, however, they were more optimistic about being better sexual partners. One woman who had begun to believe that sex was no longer for her was helped to a realization that it could be, and she became a changed person almost overnight.

A recent—and continuing—study of middle-class couples in their forties and fifties conducted by the adult-development program of the Langley Porter Neuropsychiatric Institute at the medical center of the University of California has found that 70 to 80 per cent of the fifty couples studied were "pretty happy" to "very happy" with their lives in general but that their feelings about their sex lives seemed a little clouded. Although many of the men rated their sex lives as about the same as or better than in the earlier days of their marriages, their wives gave either negative or ambiguous responses.

In *Married Love in the Middle Years*, Dr. James A. Peterson emphasized that sexual success in middle age is extremely important for both partners. He considers it important not so much as a means of relieving pent-up drives, which are a characteristic of adolescence, but more as a symbol of the tie between two people who have come to love one another deeply. In other words, the function of sex in the middle years, as far as Dr. Peterson is concerned, is to serve as an affirmation of love and tenderness and a symbol of togetherness.

Sexual intercourse in the late forties and fifties, he tells us, probably will not be marked with as much passion as it was in the early days of a marriage, but what it lacks in fire it gains in depth. Perhaps the fire has been banked, he said, but a warm glow remains; sexual relations may be different from what they have been, but they can be just as rewarding.

YES, THERE IS HOPE

Other doctors and behavioral scientists have produced a growing body of research, complete with case histories, that makes a strong case for continued—and satisfying—sexuality into old age. There is no automatic cutoff date; sexual interests, needs, and abilities can continue to play important roles in life, whether one is single or married, male or female.

Unfortunately, our cultural attitudes are such that they have inhibited the middle-aged and elderly in expressing themselves sexually and have triggered unnecessary feelings of guilt, self-incrimination, and inadequacy. Women especially have suffered from their inhibitions as well as from the mistaken notion that menopause is a punctuation mark ending femininity and sexuality. All "the change" really means is that the reproductive years are over; it certainly does not need to signal the end of the enjoyment of sex or of having sex appeal. This was emphasized to us recently when a dynamic woman in her early fifties returned from a trip abroad and confided that not one but two men had expressed an interest in making love to her. Although she rejected both offers, her morale was boosted, for being propositioned in that way had meant to her that she was still desirable.

She, like many other women, had been equating love, romance, and sex with youth. One reason for this was that her children, like many others, had voiced skepticism about their parents' love life, finding it difficult to accept the fact that older couples continue to have intercourse or find it enjoyable. This attitude sometimes carries over to the couples themselves, as Karl Bowman, the psychiatrist, pointed out when he observed that men and women may refrain from seeking sexual relations or remarriage after the loss of a spouse because "even they themselves have come to regard sex as a little ridiculous."

Many who have studied sexual responses among older people are in agreement that intercourse can provide an important psychological and physiological outlet as the years advance. The late Lawrence K. Frank, psychologist and author of *The Conduct of Sex,* wrote that the opportunity for sexual relations is an important primary source of psychological reinforcement for some older people, particularly for men at a time when they face the loss of the prestige and self-confidence that accompanied their work and for women when they fear a diminution of attractiveness and desirability following menopause.

To Dr. Alvin F. Goldfarb, associate professor of obstetrics and gynecology at Jefferson Medical College in Philadelphia, sexuality is far more than a psychological reinforcement. He regards it as a reflection of the total well-being of a middle-aged woman—the results of past experiences and present family life. It is his further observation that problems of sexuality can be linked to other concerns—general health, emotional outlook, or relations in the home.

During the generations in which society downgraded or ignored a woman's need for sexual activity after her childbearing years had ended, there was created a denigrating stereotype of the "sexless older years," in the view of the late Isadore Rubin, a longtime editor of *Sexology* magazine. He attributed this to a tendency to think of aging as a disease rather than a normal process and to the fact that most studies had dealt with older people in hospitals or institutions rather than with a broad spectrum of the aging still in or on the edge of the mainstream of life.

There has been a tendency to assume that most women over forty today are still caught in the "cultural bind" of Victorianism that plagued their grandmothers and great-grandmothers, and even their mothers; but as women have progressed through the twentieth century, they have come a long way by changing their own attitudes toward sex at all ages, including the middle years. Holdovers from the past do persist, of course, as demonstrated in a survey conducted by *Psychology Today* magazine to measure romanticism and sexual liberalism. Of the more than twenty thousand responses to one hundred questions about sexual practices and attitudes, only 9 per cent were from men and women over forty-five. Among the replies was a particularly revealing letter from a woman who wrote: "I lost my first husband when I was forty-five years old, the second, after only three weeks' honeymoon, at forty-eight. what happens to a woman such as I, wanting, 'sex, copulation, love,' but wanting it only within the 'proper Victorian bounds,' yet feeling very wanton and very bad at times? Nights, days, weeks, months, with no opportunity to meet a man or men can be so eroding, it is sad and frightening. I am one who is starved beyond endurance."

SEX EDUCATION FOR MOM AND DAD

Many adults are woefully ignorant about sex, despite years of experience. Some may be less knowledgeable than their children because of the revolution in sex education in our schools, where the birds and the bees have been supplanted by clinical data. While this will be beneficial to the next generation of parents, formal classroom indoctrination has come too late for most of the rest of us. Yet it really is never too late to get a good grounding in the facts of life from doctors or from books. This is particularly true of women confronted with what many of them look upon as the mysteries of middle age; apprehensions generated by the menopause, as we have seen, can be obviated or at least alleviated with a little foreknowledge. And it should go without saying that the middle-aged generation is sexually ignorant despite its years of experience.

Marriage counselors, physicians, psychologists, and family-life authorities recognize the need for sex education for the mature and young alike. In the past this teaching, geared to adolescents, was limited to the reproductive aspects of sex. Very little was said about human sexual behavior until researchers such as Kinsey and Masters and Johnson and the host of writers who have interpreted their studies came along to fill the void.

Dr. David R. Reuben, the psychiatrist who wrote the best seller *Everything You Always Wanted to Know About Sex, But Were Afraid to Ask*, maintains that adults in their forties and fifties know more about their automobiles or golf clubs than they do about sex and sexuality. "When you buy an automobile," he says, "they give you a wonderful book that tells you how to turn the key and what to do if something goes wrong. Most people find out about sex through on-the-job training. They start in with sex about fourteen or fifteen. They make mistakes for about thirty years. By the time they really get the hang of it, it's already too late."

A woman needs all the information she can get about every aspect of sex, according to Dr. Reuben. He recommends frank discussions between husband and wife and prescribes that both consult professionals who will be sympathetic and understanding. "A woman who is losing sexual contact with her husband has the most difficult problem that a woman can face," Dr. Reuben explained, "and yet one that can be solved if she will apply the time, effort and energy to resolve it."

Physicians have become more open and receptive with their belated recognition of the extent of sexual ignorance and sexual problems. They are trying to do something about it by offering guidance to their patients. The new open-mindedness about sex is reflected in discussions of sex at scientific conferences that are encouraging patients to look upon their doctors as a source of advice and counsel.

In other words, says Dr. Joshua Goldin, assistant professor of psychiatry at the University of California School of Medicine, sexual topics have come out in the open.

"We're not forbidden in the same way we used to be to acknowledge that there are sexual problems for older people—problems having to do with normal heterosexual relations, difficulties pertaining to impotency, frigidity, premature ejaculation, and so on. By routinely inquiring of the patients about their sexual lives, and by working to develop an attitude of being open-minded, nonjudgmental, and nonpunitive about sex, we can encourage them to communicate with us about their sexual maladjustments and thus educate them."

Some mature people are inhibited in their sex lives because they came out of traditionally repressive and inhibitive environments, but they are beginning to recognize that normal, healthy, reasonable people engage in sexual intercourse after forty, according to Dr. Goldin. "They no longer feel guilty about what they are doing," he added, "nor do they deprive themselves of those experiences. Often it becomes more permissible, more comfortable to acknowledge the fact that they're having sexual maladjustments because it's very common. Then, too, the possibility exists that these things can be corrected."

As for formal sex education for adults, P. K. Houdek, director of the Kansas City Social Health Society, reports that adult audiences often ask him to lecture on "Sex and Age." And Dr. Gerald Neubeck, who teaches sex education to college students, believes that older adults would profit from the same kind of instruction. Of course, teaching methods would have to be adapted to the values and experiences of the forty-year-old, which are different from those of the youth of twenty, but the basic information certainly would have to be the same.

Dr. Ashley Montagu, the anthropologist, advocates sex education for everyone but adds his own characteristic barb with the declaration that "if you were really trained in the art of being a human being, you wouldn't need to have any education in sex because of your sense of responsibility and your awareness of the vulnerability of the other human being." He accuses what he judges to be "a vast number of people" of being "utterly incompetent" in matters of sex. "They have never learned," he explained, "they have never been taught. They pick up these things from their friends and dirty talk, and all sorts of unfortunate ways, so that they often experience rejections even when they are willing to do what is required, because of their awkwardness and crudity."

A fifty-seven-year-young widow echoed these sentiments in a letter to *Psychology Today,* responding to the sex quiz it conducted among its subscribers. She declared that research should dispel the "fog of ignorance" about sex. "In the age when we can go to the moon, something constructive ought to be done in teaching man about woman and woman about man and doctors about both. The hostility between men and women over unsatisfactory sex experiences is unbelievable."

Jhan and June Robbins's report on Masters and Johnson's educational techniques presents another view of sex education: "There is more delight in sex for a couple who have learned it and each other, as there is more delight in the cello for someone who has learned to play it."

Dr. Walter Stokes, a psychiatrist who has practiced in Washington, D.C., for more than thirty-five years, specializing in marriage and family life and problems related to sex, is optimistic about the enjoyment of sex by future generations. He maintains, however, that for true sexual gratification in the later years, people should first have enjoyed it when they were young.

SEX AND THE WOMAN ALONE

Sex, or the lack of it, emerges as one of the principal problems of the woman alone—whether she has been married or has remained single. (See also Chapter 6.) Dr. Reuben received so many letters from women asking what they should do about sex that he devoted his next book to the subject. "I am convinced," he wrote in *McCall's* magazine (February 1971), "that women have unique sexual problems—problems that require a fresh approach if there is to be any hope of solving them. The concept of a woman as a second-rate man still lingers on in the thinking of too many otherwise well-educated men (and some women)."

For centuries women have been limited to two socially acceptable alternatives—marriage or spinsterhood (spinsterhood as we use it means chastity). Isn't it about time for them to have the same options and opportunities as men? And for older women to have the same options that are now open to younger women, who have adopted more liberal attitudes toward sex, particularly before marriage, and feel less guilty about their amours? Dr. Carlfred B. Broderick, a professor of family relations at Pennsylvania State University, attributed the changing feminine view largely to a general increase in the freedom and responsibility of women in all areas of life. He has some concern lest the freer life-style will endanger social institutions such as the church and family, but he also contends that changing sexual mores have not been accompanied by a rise in promiscuity; his studies indicate, rather, that most of the increase in premarital sex has involved couples going steady or engaged.

The late Dr. Richard H. Klemer, chairman of child development and family relations at the University of North Carolina at Greensboro, examined the subject of unmarried women and their motivations in an article in *Medical Aspects of Human Sexuality* (April 1969) entitled "Problems of Widowed, Divorced, and Unmarried Women." He found that some women are "delighted" with the sexual freedom that accompanies remaining single—

"freedom for more sex as well as freedom from too much." Most women who saw him for counseling were fearful, however, lest they establish reputations for being promiscuous. "It isn't that they don't want sex—many of them are passionately eager," he said. "But most want some sort of emotional commitment to go along with it. They don't want to be 'used' and they feel demeaned by the this-for-that type of sex bargain. It is still true that most American women have been conditioned to a strong sex-love association. For many, relying on other forms of sexual release is preferable to casual intercourse with a relative stranger, regardless of any new freedom."

Basically, Dr. Klemer's counsel to the unmarried woman to help her through middle age was that she must learn to accept the probability and even the desirability of remaining single and still living successfully or, alternately, of improving her relationships with other people and becoming motivated to seek male companionship so that she may have a good chance of finding a husband. While the first option seemed "simpler and safer," he felt that choosing it would be to ignore the statistical fact that even at thirty-five a woman who has never married still has a better than fifty-fifty chance of finding a mate; at forty the figure is 20 per cent, and at forty-five it is 12 per cent. The remarriage rates for divorcées and widows are much higher.

If a woman chooses the first alternative—remaining single—she should not ignore the fact that her life will be enriched if she improves her social skills. Dr. Klemer urged the second alternative, through which a woman can learn to evaluate herself, gain self-confidence, and set some realistic goals. Because many perennial bachelor girls have rationalized their situations, it can be difficult to help them to an honest self-appraisal. Some maintain that they have remained single because of obligations to aged parents; others protest that they have never had a chance to meet men—or the *right* men. While such claims can be valid, they are more often excuses than reasons for remaining single.

"Many of the women who talk about their obligations don't bother to add that they were emotionally dependent on their father and mother even before those parents became their dependents," Klemer observed. "They just couldn't leave emotionally when they could have left financially.

"And it is true that there are a few women who have lived such isolated lives that they didn't really have a fair opportunity to meet other men. But most modern women come within meeting distance of enough eligible males in a week's time to provide them with all the dates and love affairs they might need, if they could only meet and relate to those men."

The most inhibiting factor when it comes to meeting men, in Dr. Klemer's opinion, is the woman's own feeling of self-worth—or lack of it. Many who do not meet men have very low self-esteem and are convinced that anyone they encounter will not like them. This makes them so standoffish or so overly eager to impress that men really do react negatively. "On the other hand," Dr. Klemer added, "women who do have self-confidence don't have to spend all their time thinking 'What is he thinking now?' or 'I wonder if I look all right.' Instead, they can think about what they could be doing to help the man to be more comfortable in the situation. Consequently, he likes them and they are even better at relating to the next person."

Dr. Klemer found it necessary to help the older woman achieve a higher sense of self-worth than she needed as a teen-ager, principally because of the blows to morale inflicted by our youth-conscious society. "They are made to feel so inferior by our colossal commercial promotion of the attractiveness of college-age girls," he said, "that their self-confidence begins to waver. Once this happens, they are in fact less attractive."

In the final analysis, Klemer found that the most important step for the single woman seeking to create a deep love relationship with a man will be to become emotionally indispensable to him. "A curious fallacy held by many people, including many older unmarried people, is that they can get someone to fall in love with them by being so irresistibly fascinating that the other person cannot help himself," he explained. "This is nonsense. People fall in love and stay in love because they have an emotional need for the other person."

When we asked Ann Landers, who conducts the widely syndicated letters column, about the moral standards of the single middle-aged woman, she expressed the conviction that there is no radical change of values in middle age —that, indeed, a woman's moral standards are about what they were when she was a teen-ager.

"A girl who has her head on straight is not about to fall in bed with the first fellow who brings up the subject when she has been widowed or divorced," Miss Landers replied. "On the other hand, a girl who has been loose all of her dating years and even perhaps through marriage, if she is divorced, will maintain the same standards that she has always had.

"Some women write and ask me if I feel they should lower their standards a little because 'I'm alone; I do want to get married. What do you think?' Well, I think this. I believe that no man would drop a woman that he really cared about or was truly interested in because she didn't go to bed with him. I think this is an excuse some women use. I have heard many divorcées say, 'Well, I would rather sit home than go out with these eight-handed idiots that I have been running into. I have to defend myself on the second date and I am sick of it.'

"Well, I don't buy it. I think that if a woman has something to offer, she can hold a man's interest without going to bed with him. I do believe that if a woman is, say, forty-one years of age and has been married and now is either widowed or divorced, and she goes with a man for, say several months, if she cares about him and he cares about her, I don't think she is going to burn in hell if she does go to bed with him. At that age I would imagine that there might be something wrong with the woman who could go with a man—a woman who has been married and is accustomed to some sexual relationship—to go with a man month after month and not have some close relationship. It would seem to me that she would be some neurotic personality because this is a very normal, natural thing, particularly if it is an outgrowth of having spent a great deal of time together.

"I know that I will be criticized for this but I try to be realistic. I try to give advice that is livable. People are not plaster saints. They are humans and they have certain needs, certain desires, and I think that for a woman who has had a good marriage and a good sexual relationship with a man, it would be unnatural to go with a man she really cared about and who cared about her for a year and not go to bed with him."

Like Ann Landers and other columnists, the Information Center on the Mature Woman, in New York, receives a considerable volume of mail from women asking questions about sex. One wrote, for example:

"After twenty-seven wonderful years of marriage, I was widowed fourteen months ago. Recently I accepted a date because the man looked 'safe' and I thought it would be a wonderful evening. But before the night was over I felt like a lawyer trying to win my first case. My companion felt I should not have accepted the date in the first place if I didn't expect sex.

"Other men I've met at work have also asked me out and suggested the same thing. Why is it when you mention the word *widow* or *divorcée,* the first thing that comes to a man's mind is free sex? There must be men on this earth in my age group (I am forty-eight but look much younger) who are looking for a decent woman. Do you think the way I feel is wrong?"

The answer was reassuring: "Not at all, but the world is changing and so are attitudes about sex. People today tend to be much more open about these things. Why not accept those dates, while at the same time making the men aware as subtly and indirectly as you can that you're not going to fall into bed immediately just because someone buys you a dinner or takes you to a movie. Stick to your guns and your standards. You'll find someone who appreciates them."

LOVE AND SEX

A writer to an advice column posed this question not long ago: "I am forty-five and my husband is forty-eight. We get along just fine and have for years. But lately there's been so much talk about marriage manuals and how-to books on sex, I wonder if we're missing something. Do you think we should buy one?"

The reply pointed out that many troubled couples had read three or four marriage manuals without finding happiness in them. It went on to quote John Fowles, the novelist, who wrote: "To teach the physiology of sex without the psychology of love is to teach all about a ship except how to steer it."

The recent spate of popularly written "how-to" books about sexuality has raised a basic question for consideration by people of all ages: what is the distinction between love and sex? In his discussion *Love and Will,* Dr. Rollo May, the psychiatrist, maintains that the highly vaunted American sexual freedom has become a new form of Puritanism, consisting of three elements: alienation from the body, separation of emotion from reason, and use of the body as a machine. In other words, a kind of depersonalization of sex has occurred. Dr. May fears that the resultant unromantic technical preoccupation with sex may rob a woman of what she wants most physically and emotionally, "the man's spontaneous abandon at the moment of climax," which in turn gives her the ecstasy of which she is capable.

"When we cut through all the rigamarole about roles and performance," Dr. May writes, "what still remains is how amazingly important the sheer act of intimacy of relationship is—the meeting, the growing closeness with the excitement of not knowing where it will lead, the assertion of self, and the giving of the self—in making a sexual encounter memorable." Dr. May expanded on his ideas in an interview in which he advocated a greater knowledge of love than of sex. He has no quarrel with the findings of scientists such as Masters and Johnson because they apply technology to sexual relationships. "The more we learn about sex, the better," Dr. May declared, despite his conviction that sex is only one part of the true marital relationship. "What people need and want is intimacy and authentic love."

Derek Wright, the British psychologist, who finds all of us tyrannized by sexual "liberation," agrees with Dr. May that sex becomes "a meaningless aside, a cul-de-sac," when looked upon as an isolated human function. "We find meaning," he adds, "not in some limited purpose it is said to serve, not as procreation or mental health, but through becoming aware of that whole texture of connectedness within which the sexual is only one component. True sexual liberation occurs when the sexual is dissolved into the fully personal and when sexual ideologies are discarded for the tedious pedantries they are."

Sex relations, therefore, are important to all women—

particularly the mature woman—not only for the pleasure received but for the *quality* of intimacy the relationship communicates, as well as for ego support. Sex can provide these only if it is accompanied by tenderness. As Dr. May observes, it is a strange thing in our society that what goes into building a relationship—the sharing of tastes, fantasies, dreams, hopes for the future, and the fallout of fears from the past—tends to make people more vulnerable when going to bed together. "They are more wary," he says, "of the tenderness that goes with psychological and spiritual nakedness than they are of the physical nakedness of sexual intimacy."

SEX AND MENOPAUSE

Five common causes of sexual problems during and after menopause are cited by Dr. Alvin Goldfarb as fear of pregnancy, loss of libido, painful intercourse (dyspareunia), family discord, and the kind of fatigue that often accompanies aging.

Fear of pregnancy can, of course, be allayed with the use of sophisticated contraceptive methods until a woman is certain she can no longer conceive (usually a year after the last menstrual period). A decline in libido may be related indirectly to diminished production of hormones as well as to other factors of middle age. Physiological results of estrogen deprivation such as flashes, night sweats, insomnia, and fatigue can also interfere with sexual responsiveness. Alleviating discomfort through estrogen-replacement therapy may enable a woman to enjoy the physical relationship again.

One nagging physical problem common among women after menopause, according to Dr. Sherwin Kaufman, is a gradual thinning and drying of vaginal tissue, usually attributed to estrogen deprivation, which can make intercourse painful. A normal vagina is moist, soft, and elastic; with advancing years, it begins to tighten, and the vaginal lips become thin and shrunken and the lining rough and sometimes ulcerated. Itching, irritation, and either a discharge or dryness are the symptoms of what is known as atrophic vaginitis.

"Once the diagnosis of atrophic vaginitis is made," Dr. Kaufman said, "treatment is specific. The simplest therapy is estrogen applied locally, in the form of cream or estrogen suppositories. Estrogen by mouth may be used instead or in addition. Improvement is dramatically fast. Within a week or two the vaginal tissues change from a tender, thin, brittle state to the normally moist, thicker, more elastic, nontender state. But this treatment must always be under medical supervision."

Atrophic vaginitis is the frequent diagnosis of another expert, Dr. Robert W. Kistner, assistant professor of gynecology and obstetrics at the Harvard University Medical School. He has been finding increasing numbers of cases of vasomotor symptoms, such as hot flashes, and atrophic vaginitis among patients who come to him for relief from painful intercourse. Many more women could enjoy their sex lives for years after menopause if knowledge of simple therapeutic measures was more widespread.

Some gynecological diseases affecting sexuality during and after menopause are treated surgically. The physician's first task in these cases is to explain the procedure and its implications carefully to dispel unnecessary fears. Many couples believe, for example, that a hysterectomy spells the end of sex for a woman. This need not be true; the level of a woman's sexual response will continue unchanged if she has been properly prepared psychologically for what is going to happen. A hysterectomy involving the removal of the ovaries will bring about what is called artificial menopause, but this can be alleviated through the same hormone therapy that is available to women going through a normal change of life.

THE LAST EGG IN THE BASKET —THE CHANGE-OF-LIFE BABY

Fears of conceiving unwanted babies after the age of fifty persist despite the fact that pregnancy is highly unlikely then. So rare are births to women over fifty that the National Bureau of Vital Statistics no longer reports them as a separate item. In the last year in which these "change-of-life babies" were reported, the total for the United States was a mere eighty-two. Among women forty-five to forty-nine the reported births were only about eight hundred for the entire country, although women in their forties are usually able to conceive.

Dr. Stuart Oster, assistant attending obstetrician and gynecologist at the Women's Hospital Division of St. Luke's Hospital Center in New York, tabulated the ages of new mothers in New York and found that 2.2 per cent of the 150,000 babies delivered in one year were born to women over forty. Of seventy-nine women over forty he interviewed in his family-planning clinic, only one indicated that she had wanted to have another child; the others had hoped that they had completed their families and said that their last pregnancies had been unplanned —and unwanted.

In explaining their conditions, they told Dr. Oster that they had been convinced that "at my age I wouldn't have a child" or "I hadn't conceived in so many years, why now?" or "oh, yes, I used to use contraceptives, but I didn't think I needed to at this late age." He urges any woman over forty who does not want to become pregnant to use some form of contraception until the menopause is over.

Dr. Kistner agrees, explaining that premenopausal women often are misled by irregular periods into the erroneous belief that they are no longer fertile. But, he warns, "the last egg in the basket could lead to pregnancy —wanted or unwanted." "Many women feel that over the age of forty-five they don't ovulate," he added, "and many of them don't. They may be having irregular periods, but that 'last egg' could still be there. If a woman happens to have intercourse at the time she ovulates, she can become pregnant."

To avoid unexpected—and often unwelcome and tragic —pregnancies, many doctors recommend family-planning measures. For women on the verge of menopause the birth-control pill sometimes serves a dual purpose: It prevents the conception and relieves the distress of premenopausal symptoms caused by hormonal imbalance. The pill does not delay menopause, however, and once it is over, contraception is no longer necessary. A woman cannot be certain she is no longer ovulating until she has gone through a full year without menstruating. Once menstruation has ceased and menopause has occured, Dr. Kistner recommends estrogen replacement therapy if indicated.

Some middle-aged women were caught in the middle of a recent controversy in Congress over the birth-control pill. The debate about whether it was safe or not caused many to panic and turn to other methods of contraception such as the intrauterine device, the diaphragm, or the rhythm method. Dr. Elizabeth B. O'Connell, director of research and development in family planning at the International Institute for the Study of Human Reproduction at Columbia University, reported that a wave of unwanted pregnancies resulted, leading to disrupted homes and careers, illegal abortions, and some "statistically certain deaths."

She deplored what she called the artificial creation of

two camps of doctors as a result of the pill controversy. Most doctors managed to stay out of both camps, she added, by accepting arguments of each. They were pro-pill "in the sense that we recognized the inherent value of these drugs, when properly used," she explained, and antipill when considering specific patients who should not use this method of contraception for medical reasons.

Dr. Oster holds out hope to the women who dread the "closing of the gates" to fertility and hope for a last chance at motherhood before their ovaries cease functioning. "I don't think there are any particular dangers in a woman over forty having a child," he said. "If she wants one, she should first visit her physician for a complete checkup. He can determine whether she can carry a child without undue complications."

There are some dangers, particularly the risk of bearing a defective child. Medical scientists have produced statistical evidence in recent years showing that the chances that a woman will produce a mongoloid increase with age; the older the mother, the more likely she and her husband are to be confronted with this tragedy. The specter of mongolism apparently is not a major deterrent to belated pregnancies, but it is something every woman should think about seriously before deciding on motherhood after forty.

Although our society is moving toward earlier marriages and earlier motherhood (half of all couples have had their last child by the time the mother is twenty-six), some women deliberately postpone childbearing. There are those, of course, who marry late in life, while others enter second marriages after forty; in both instances it is natural for a woman to want to have a child with her husband. The new fertility drugs enhance the chances of becoming pregnant even at a time when the possibility of conception is beginning to diminish.

Dr. Albert Higdon, attending obstetrician-gynecologist

at Holy Name Hospital in Teaneck, New Jersey, finds less risk for the woman over forty and her baby if she has previously borne children than for the woman of the same age who is delivering for the first time. He made a study of six hundred mothers over forty, including his private patients and others treated at the hospital, over a period of eight years, and reached the conclusion that today's women are younger physiologically than were their mothers or grandmothers; they even appear younger than their chronological age might indicate. Therefore, he reasoned, they are probably better able to bear children at an older age; they also receive better prenatal care than was available in the past. "It's more of a pleasure to take care of a woman having her first baby over forty because this is a very exciting time of her life," he said. "She makes a good patient, and the reason is that she has had forty years to mature."

MEN HAVE PROBLEMS TOO

Women are not alone in going through a physical transition that affects their sex lives during middle age. Men undergo changes that create a real crisis for some. Panic may set in when a man experiences his first episode of impotence, which sometimes leads to an extramarital affair in a desperate effort to gain reassurance about his virility and masculinity. Impotence at this time of life—or any other, for that matter—can result from tension, anxiety, or pressure on the job; the extra drain on emotional energies leaves nothing for sex.

In *Everything You Always Wanted to Know About Sex*, Dr. Reuben maintains that some men who suffer from impotence reject the idea of sex or avoid it because they are afraid of another failure. Others dabble in promiscuity in an attempt to prove to themselves that it is not they who have the problem but their wives! This can be true, for there have been cases in which wives have helped to resolve their husband's impotence through open communication accompanied by sympathy and love. Both need the reassurance of a physician that they are in good health before they start trying to analyze their problem together. They might begin by asking: "Are we sexually bored with each other?" This is a key question, for boredom appears to be a common cause of sexual failure. Masters and Johnson have helped couples overcome this handicap by seeking new stimulation and trying to be as attractive as possible to each other.

We would like to emphasize that just as a husband, through patience and understanding, is expected to help his wife through the difficult moments of the menopause, so a wise wife needs to be compassionate and sympathetic toward the problems of her middle-aged husband, even when she is having problems of her own. There are those who seem to feel that sexual intercourse is the principal way a woman can communicate love to her mate. One of them, Dr. Theodore Lidz, writing in *The Person,* said that the sex lives of many couples are more satisfactory in middle age than they were in their youth. While it may be less "frenzied," he noted, each knows the needs and unspoken signals of the other, and they have by now found ways to satisfy one another. They have greater control, perhaps, or skill or even "artistry," as Lidz put it, and they derive more "subtle pleasure" from the sexual act.

Unfortunately, some husbands and wives use sex as a weapon. A wife may withhold herself from her husband to make a bargaining point in an argument or to get something she wants. A husband might use sex as a weapon by insisting on it. He thinks that this proves he is boss or it enables him to avenge a real or fancied slight.

On the other hand, some insightful wives do everything they can to preserve a spirit and atmosphere that keep romance alive and prolong a successful marital sex life. They try to keep their homes free of dissension, and they work at staying physically fit and attractive—yes, even seductive. And they may go so far as to "set the scene" for marital happiness, in the manner of the wife of a newly elected governor of Pennsylvania, who refused to move into the two-million-dollar gubernatorial mansion until twin beds had been removed from the master bedroom. "We prefer a double bed," she said.

It is a common assumption that, after twenty or thirty years of marriage, a couple's sex life is likely to pall. Typical of this notion is the story about the husband who had been in a hospital for some time after suffering a coronary occlusion. On the day he went home he asked his doctor whether it would be all right to resume sexual relations. "Yes," the physician responded, "with your wife, by all means. But not with other women. I don't want you to get excited!"

An excellent booklet, *Sexual Life in the Later Years,* published by the Sex Information and Education Council of the United States (SIECUS) maintains that regularity of intercourse is the most essential factor for both men and women in retaining a capacity for effective performance. Some couples seem to look forward to the day they can find a good excuse to end sexual relations; this is particularly true among those who have always felt that sex was an unpleasant chore, as in the case of the wife who periodically asked her husband, "Are you going to use me tonight?" For the average middle-aged partners in good health who are compatible and have at least some degree of sexual interest, there can be both desire and activity for many years.

CHAPTER
4

Mirror, Mirror, on the Wall . . .

"I HAVE EVERYTHING now I had twenty years ago, except it's all lower."

With those words, the late Gypsy Rose Lee, whose figure was her fortune as an ecdysiast, summed up for most of us who are over forty how we appear to ourselves when we look into our mirrors. In other words, if we have taken care of ourselves, we are in pretty good shape—some of us are in *great* shape—and if we do perceive a few sags and bags, jowls and gray streaks, roughening skin, and other signs of the attrition of the years, there are quite a few things we can do to counteract them, if we really want to.

Arlene Francis, the actress and radio and television personality, insists that you *can* turn back the clock, "but first, you must forget about age . . . *anybody's* age. Chronological age has little to do with your physical, mental, or spiritual age." Bonnie Prudden, the physical-fitness expert, has concluded that "age begins when you slow down, *not* when you get older."

The place to begin with personal preservation and rehabilitation—and even with restoration—is with the physical self, learning first to accept what cannot be changed and then to change or minimize what can be. Of utmost importance is the need to feel good about yourself, to look at yourself through rose-colored bifocals. Look at yourself through those glasses and what you see will be reflected in the way you look to others and will motivate you to wear the right clothes and the right makeup and pursue a sensible diet and exercise routine.

We have among us, unfortunately, many women who regard it as natural to become progressively less attractive as they move through the forties and fifties; if this be the case, they may merely be reaping the harvest of misspent or *un*spent earlier years. "Women who use their talents to the full become handsome in later life," observed Catherine Drinker Bowen, the author. "They grow to a special beauty of their own."

So, you might say that pride is one key to fitness. We all have—or should have—a certain sense of self-worth, and if our self-examination shows us to be unfit, pride alone may be enough to make us want to repair the damage we see as we gaze upon ourselves in the mirror. Have you ever made a list of your good and less good points as you stand before your bathroom mirror? Take an inventory, write down what you see, and then think about what you have noted. Then, get to work! The help of experts is often needed, and there are many good books prescribing specific action. The advice and help of friends and relatives can and should be sought—and accepted if it is lovingly and constructively given. You are unlikely to get such advice without asking for it.

Meanwhile, there is no time like right now to begin a head-to-toe interior and exterior decoration program, and probably the best place to start is with your figure.

PRUNING FROM WITHIN AND WITHOUT

No one has to be told that proper diet and regular exercise can do wonders not only for appearance but also for morale. The "diet game" is being played by many to the fiscal well-being of the few who capitalize on trying to make figure control look easy and, in the process, victimize the gullible. But it is not easy. Getting into shape —and staying that way—takes hard work, perseverance, and often the cooperation of others.

A short-term diet will not usually provide a long-range solution for weight—or fat—problems of a mature woman. Neither will a program that relies heavily on drugs, medication, food fads, or constant visits to a doctor. It may require medical advice, after your regular annual physical examination, to arrive at the radical change of eating habits often called for in middle age. A doctor's help may be needed in deciding that the problem is not simply one of weight gain but more a matter of redistribution of weight during menopause. Muscle may be giving way to fat without a substantial increase in poundage. This may mean that the food one has been eating for years is now causing bulges in the wrong places. So a change in diet may be in order to emphasize muscle building as well as weight maintenance or loss. It is well known, for example, that the older we become the fewer calories we burn and therefore the less food we need to keep our furnaces stoked. By the same token, the composition of the foods may require review, with a heavier emphasis on protein and less consumption of carbohydrates.

In our research, we consulted scores of people, among them Dr. Seymour Schlussel, a leading authority on weight control. He has concluded that middle-aged women should find it easier to lose weight once they are in the menopause and no longer subject to the cyclic variations of hormones secreted by the ovaries. Bloating caused by water retention plagues many younger women before each menstrual period, causing fingers to swell and the lower abdomen to feel full, and producing nervous irritation as a result of edema of the cerebral tissues. This can, of course, be remedied with diuretic pills, prescribed by a doctor; the problem does not arise among women in and beyond menopause unless the hormones they take for their flashes contribute to water retention. But any water retained during the three-week period of taking hormones is usually lost during the week they are not taken.

"The basic ingredient in any dietary regime is a balance between the amount of food that is ingested and the amount of energy expended," Dr. Schlussel declared. There may be certain times of the month when some kinds of food should be avoided; a woman might stay away from highly spiced or salty foods before a menstrual period to minimize fluid retention, for example. It is true, however, that some women tend to be a little more lethargic during menopause, which makes it important for them to try to keep active, not only to firm up tissues but to keep from seeking refuge in food. "People may eat to compensate for other inadequacies in their life-style," Dr. Schlussel observed.

The middle-aged woman whose children have left home and who is alone a good part of the time may, indeed, become a "foodoholic," a secret eater, who gains weight to the surprise and consternation of those who observe her low consumption at the dinner table. What she really needs is the activity and self-control, as well as the motivation, that will enable her to eat less.

Hand in hand with fewer calories comes the need for more exercise. Women, and men too, tend to become lazy and neglect exercise in their forties and beyond, which adds to the middle-aged spread. Too little exercise can be as telling as eating too much of the wrong foods. Dr. Fred Allman of Atlanta, an orthopedic surgeon and member of the American Medical Association's Committee on Exercise and Physical Fitness, is convinced that the isolated elements of fitness have been exaggerated at the expense of total strength and flexibility. In addition to diet and exercise, he prescribes proper rest and relaxation for women as well as men. While he finds that the average American female of forty-five is not physically fit, he concludes that she is in better shape than her husband. This will be less and less the case, however, as women become increasingly involved in the world and work of men.

Genetic differences have seemed to protect women from premature heart attacks throughout life until the menopause, but they are beginning to suffer from cardiovascular ailments at younger ages. Dr. Allman attributes this to the fact that more women are smoking more cigarettes and are living under more pressure as they have been emancipated into many of the tension-ridden roles traditionally filled by men. However, he noted, sixty out of every hundred women still outlive their husbands.

Doctors have encountered difficulty in keeping women on fitness programs because they tend to follow such regimens only spasmodically. A woman will undertake a rigorous antibulge campaign of diet and exercise in anticipation of the swimming season, but once she has squeezed into her bathing suit, she tends to forget about the necessary maintenance.

Physical-fitness "experts" are a dime a dozen. Bonnie Prudden, one of the more successful and sensible high priestesses of fitness—who practices what she preaches by keeping herself in good condition as a grandmother in her fifties—maintains that under your epidermis, *your body is whatever you have allowed to happen to it.* She says the trouble begins at about the age of fourteen, which she considers to be the physiological threshhold of middle age for many; the basic problem is overweight, which carries with it, among other things, the poor posture that takes its toll in later years. One of the banes of middle age is kyphosis, a thickening of tissues at the back of the neck, which often occurs under stress. In such a case, the muscles tighten, begin to hurt, and become chunky and fat. "Pretty soon," Mrs. Prudden says, you look at yourself in the mirror and say, 'Oh, my God,' and then you tighten some more." She blames enlarged thighs and saddlebags of fat on the hips on emotional stress as well as too much sitting. Sagging breasts she attributes to the collapse or weakening of chest muscles. No one who exercises properly and regularly, she insists, will have Gypsy Rose Lee's complaint in that sector!

Another technical word Mrs. Prudden uses is *hypokinetic,* which simply means that you are not moving around enough, and she—and doctors, too—says that the less you exercise, the greater your chance of suffering a heart attack; the more active you are, the greater your odds of surviving one. There are also data showing that there is twice as much diabetes and much more emotional stress among inactive women.

Mrs. Prudden blames a poor appearance on five things: inactivity, stress, improper diet, jobs that are too confining, and too many tranquilizers—pills, alcohol, and cigarettes.

Another authority on health, beauty, and exercise, Sophia Delza, expounded for us on concerns after forty, maintaining that some women beyond that age have problems with their bodies not only because they have grown lazy but because they did not exercise enough even when they were young. "The woman over forty should, of course, pay more attention to herself than a growing person who has much more activity in her life," said Miss Delza, who advocates keeping the body in a constant state of stimulation. "The whole of life is movement," she added.

One of the indications that exercise is needed is a stooped walk; gravity takes over when a body has not been exercised enough. As Miss Lee said, everything moves downward. That is what advancing age causes, and it is why so many older people have bowed necks, pushing their heads turtlelike before them. "We are giving in to the force of the earth," Miss Delza said, "and our whole life we must make an effort to pull away from gravity."

Muscles become weakened without exercise. The area from the hips down carries the bulk of our weight—perhaps that is why girdles and corsets are called "foundation" garments—which means we need a strong, substantial base on which to sit. But too much sitting makes this foundation broaden and soften, with a consequent expansion of the waist as well. Backaches can stem from the resulting sloppy posture as well as from the lack of exercise.

Women of all ages, sizes, and degrees of physical agility were studied by Dr. Thomas Boslooper, a pastoral counselor and minister of the Reformed Church of Closter, New Jersey, for a report to the American Association for the Advancement of Science. He found in interviews with women and girls throughout the United States, from Miss Americas and Olympic athletes to housewives and grandmothers, that negative reactions to fitness tended to come from those who also complained about a variety of emotional and physical problems, while those who considered themselves to be in good emotional and physical health responded positively.

The mature women who complained to Boslooper about emotional distress had been very active as adolescents but had steadily tapered off until physical movement was minimal and even distasteful. They had slowed down deliberately in the mistaken notion that it would make them more "feminine" to be "soft" or because they regarded physical exercise as a mark of immaturity. The women who were healthy, attractive, and able to cope with their problems considered fitness intrinsic to femininity.

It is interesting that Boslooper found that physically active women tended to have fewer complaints about menstruation and menopause as well as pregnancy and childbirth. Women who derived satisfaction from exercise appeared to him to be living more vigorously; consequently, he advised women to select a physical activity that is interesting and rewarding and then combine it whenever possible with social, cultural, and artistic pursuits.

If the muscular, nervous, circulatory, and respiratory systems are provided with the strength they need to function smoothly and produce a more youthful and radiant appearance as well as a new zest for living, Boslooper is convinced that the end result will be an enhanced capacity for coping with life's problems, increased femininity, and the approval of society, friends, family—and husbands.

LEARNING TO WALK—AGAIN

"Me? Exercise? I get plenty doing all my own housework and pushing a grocery cart through the supermarket aisles twice a week. I'm so tired at the end of the day that a lack of exercise certainly couldn't be *my* problem!"

That is the typical housewife's characteristic response to suggestions that she consider exercising to keep her figure trim. Many women think they use their muscles adequately during the miles they walk while keeping house and shopping. They also confuse weariness with muscle sag. There is really nothing special about the kind of exercise involved in one's daily routine, however, for it merely puts the same old machinery to the same mundane tasks and leaves a large part of the body lying fallow. Pushing a vacuum cleaner may require flexing of the right arm, but it leaves the left hanging idle. Loading a dishwasher or lifting a load of wet wash into the drier could hardly qualify as waist-trimming calisthenics. Even walking up and down stairs a few times a day offers no particular advantage unless executed in a special way.

In other words, to get maximum results from exercise, you need to do something *extra* each day, such as parking your car half a mile from your destination and walking the rest of the way—and back—or going up and down stairs a few extra times a day with exaggerated movements. As you hurry through the house to answer the telephone or doorbell, reach for the ceiling to stretch your abdominal muscles. But most important, learn to walk—again. Really walk, outdoors, as far as you can, as briskly as you are able, for as long as you can keep it up.

"We do not do nearly enough walking," says Marie McCormack, education director of the Information Center on the Mature Woman. "If we would all learn to walk again, to walk whenever we have the opportunity, instead of looking on walking as something that we do only when we have to, we would find that walking is a pleasurable, healthful experience, once we get out and begin to do it."

Swimming and walking probably are the best all-around exercises. Walking is the most practical, for one can engage in it almost anywhere, any time, and at any age. It requires no special skill and no equipment beyond a comfortable pair of shoes. It costs nothing. And it does not call for the involvement of another person, although a companion does add to the enjoyment. There is no doubt that a brisk walk, taken regularly, will make a person feel better and sleep more soundly; and while it might not contribute measurably to losing weight, it can help keep the figure within desirable dimensions.

Ruth Goode, coauthor with Aaron Sussman of *The*

Magic of Walking and a very active grandmother, believes that it is time for people to rediscover their feet, to go out and see the world at three miles an hour instead of at jet speeds. She adheres to the prescription of Dr. Paul Dudley White, the noted heart specialist, that the well-paced walk covers a mile in about twenty minutes. Dr. White says your heart gets maximum benefits from this rate of locomotion. Digestion, elimination, and tensions of all kinds are helped by walking, which also stimulates the muscles in the lower part of the body—what he calls our "second heart." Dr. White acknowledges that you will not lose weight in a twenty-minute walk—or even an hour-long hike—but your appetite will not be whetted either. In fact, you may eat less, he reasons, for a walk is an antidote for boredom and depression, two of the principal reasons for overeating.

Another walking enthusiast is Manya Kahn, who not only helps women to health and beauty in her New York salon but also urges them to get outdoors on their feet. She insists that it is the best single form of exercise for anyone, regardless of age or sex. Even in her salon Miss Kahn shuns ordinary gymnastics, which she maintains pile muscle on top of muscle, adding to overall girth. The reverse can be true in a coordinated routine of deep-breathing, stretching, and relaxing, she said. "American women are very figure conscious," Miss Kahn went on. "The only difficulty is that they are not too enlightened on the subject. I try to educate women in the importance of corrective diet and corrective exercise, but the most important thing is relaxation."

ON-THE-JOB EXERCISES FOR HOUSEWIVES

Many of the middle-aged women who take their problems to Miss Kahn have poor posture—rounded shoulders, caved-in chests, fatty clumps on the napes of their necks, all a result of weakened abdomens and diaphragms. The first basic routine she recommends is to lie supine on the floor and lift the legs, unbent, as high as possible or in a bent-knee-to-chest action. Either way the muscles in the abdomen and lower back return to work. Although one might start with two minutes of exercise every two or three hours, to make the effort worthwhile, Miss Kahn feels, the time should be expanded to at least thirty minutes—and ideally an hour—every day at any time except immediately after meals.

Bonnie Prudden finds that housework can be beneficial to the figure only if chores are performed with deliberate stretching motions. Exaggerated reaching and stretching and extra trips up and down stairs can help, and she likes to do her tasks to the rhythm of music on the radio or phonograph. She has isolated a few trouble spots that do not lend themselves to exercise—heavy thighs, fatty shoulders, and saddlebags on the hips. Those, she has discovered, can be more effectively countered by devoting two or three minutes a night to kneading them to increase circulation and decrease the fat. For the desk-bound office worker, she recommends tightening the buttock muscles every time a sheet of paper is removed from the typewriter or when the phone rings. This helps to counteract stenographer's spread, which results from keeping one's bottom immobilized for too long under the full weight of the body.

Many women complain to Sophia Delza that calisthenics are boring. Their only interest is in becoming thin instead of becoming more supple, strong, and happy; improving their circulation; and stimulating their minds. What does she regard as helpful exercise? Here are a few suggestions.

Hanging from a tree would, of course, be the ideal exercise for the woman with fat upper arms and dowager's hump, but since that is not feasible for most, she recommends a mini-pushup. Sit in a chair and grip the arms, pushing down on the palms of your hands to lift yourself up. Do this five or six times whenever you find yourself in a chair with arms and there is no one around who will think you have just lost your mind.

If the chair is armless, grasp the seat with your fingertips and hold your breath while trying to lift the chair as you perch on it. Do this three or four times and you will feel it in your shoulders and upper arms.

For a more supple neck and shoulders, sit erect, but not in one posture for more than ten minutes at a time. A slight periodic shifting keeps the body alert.

Calf muscles can be stimulated by removing your shoes and rotating your feet, heels on the floor and toes up.

The back and abdomen feel the benefits of pushing the small of the back against the back of a chair. Then lean forward and rest your head on your knees, stretching the body upward, arching the back into a curve and then sinking back into the chair again.

The midriff bulge calls first for dieting and then easy exercise. A saleswoman who is on her feet all day might adopt the habit of stooping frequently to pick up something—or pretending to do so. The housewife might develop the practice of stretching her hands above her head with her fingers entwined as she walks from room to room. While the hands are still clasped, she should turn her palms upward toward the ceiling, a form of stretching that can be felt from head to toe. Another "stretcher" involves moving belongings to places that are a little difficult to reach—lingerie in the lowest drawer so you have to bend to get it, and small grocery staples on the top shelves requiring a stretch to reach them.

These suggestions are scarcely enough to put a dent in one's surface; they are intended to give an idea of what a person can do, relatively easily, to help herself get ahead of herself—and stay there—in the battle of the bulges. The suggestions may motivate you to seek additional helpful hints of things that you can do on your own without a big capital outlay.

The improvement in morale that results from exercise of almost any kind is an added intangible that can lead to motivations in other areas. And while you are working on your figure, you might consider one of the oldest forms of physical culture in the world.

WHERE EAST MEETS WEST

Yoga has become a universal form of exercise. Exercise techniques developed thousands of years ago by Eastern sages have been adopted widely in the West, with students and housewives among the foremost practitioners. Ruth Bluestone Simon told us that when she started to teach yoga thirty years ago, she never gave it that label, for "it was a dirty word then that meant something for fools and charlatans. It wasn't, of course, but that was the attitude. But in the last ten or twelve years, people have come to understand about it."

There is nothing weird or occult about yoga; it is simply a natural way to improve health and appearance. It may not be widely known that there are various kinds of yoga for developing spiritual and mental well-being as well as physical stamina. Most Westerners practice hatha-yoga, which combines exercise with controlled breathing in such a way as to help maintain health.

Mrs. Simon has found one of the greatest benefits from yoga exercises in the fact that it maintains the circulation of blood through the muscles, ligaments, and even the joints, which is why many practitioners stand on their heads.

There is an old yoga saying, "You are as old as your

joints," Mrs. Simon pointed out, maintaining that the exercise keeps the joints young. People often ask her, "What's so great about being able to stand on your head?" She responds by explaining that "when you turn upside down, the blood goes into the head, into the brain, into the sinuses, into the throat, even into the chest, and blood carries with it a healing process for the body." As a fringe benefit, it improves the complexion.

There are eighty-four yoga positions—one for nearly every part of the body. Mrs. Simon encourages women to devote about thirty minutes a day to learning to do some of these to strengthen their bodies and adapt yoga movements to their everyday lives. "You get wonderful relaxation, which is just as important as the exercise itself," she said. "I won't say it's the most important thing, but for our modern way of living, it's as important as the circulatory benefits. Through yoga you can get a wonderful peacefulness, and you'll find it can even help you change your attitude toward the things that are happening to you."

WINNING THE SKIN GAME

While it may be that yoga can help improve the complexion, any kind of exercise, particularly walking, is beneficial to the skin by stimulating circulation and providing exposure to the air and to temperature changes. A warm day can be a real pore opener, a walk in the snow an astringent. What happens to your skin in the out-of-doors calls for a little more attention in front of the mirror, morning and night, and the regular use of a moisturizer, but the woman who walks, or engages in any other kind of exercise, has a chance of having a better complexion and skin tone than the one who remains quietly indoors hiding behind layers of cosmetics.

A cautionary note should be injected early and vehemently into any discussion of complexion. It is impossible to place too much emphasis on the necessity of avoiding prolonged exposure to the sun. A tan may be fashionable, particularly as a badge of a visit to an exotic resort, but what it does to the skin ranges from nuisance to tragedy. A sunburn serves to compound a problem that is built in to middle age—dryness. Premature wrinkling and a leathery texture are the two main products of suntans, and skin cancer is not uncommon among sun worshippers.

Skin tends to become thinner in the second forty, with slight surface wrinkles developing, because the skin loses water, which means it no longer has the resilience of youth. Because American women are not properly educated in beauty care, skin that might remain young for a long time starts deteriorating before middle age. Diet and age have something to do with it, of course, but the principal difficulty is that women do not know what the skin means and how to deal with it.

Cleanliness is of utmost importance. Clean skin breathes. This does not necessarily mean that the face must be scrubbed, but it should be cleansed night and morning with soap, cream, or other cleanser. Sometimes it needs more than one good going-over.

Every woman owes it to herself to try to find out what kind of skin she has, and if she cannot determine it for herself, she should ask a dermatologist or some other expert. One test involves taking the skin between the thumb and index finger to feel how thick it is. If it seems thin, it may be filled with clogged pores, which means it is oily. If it is almost like taffeta, it is too dry. Either extreme usually is the result of improper attention—or the lack of any attention at all.

Skin care begins inside with proper diet, including eight glasses of water or other nonfattening liquids a day, and plenty of sleep. Dr. Robert L. Day, assistant dean of the School of Pharmacy at the University of Southern

California, finds that most mature women with dry skin have either undergone years of exposure to the sun, *over*-emphasized cleanliness by scrubbing too hard, or suffer from a shortage of estrogens during menopause. He advises those living in low-humidity areas to avoid face powder, which speeds skin dryness, and to wash their faces only once a day, preferably at night, using lotions at other times. He also recommends the use of the least expensive and most easily applied cosmetics for dry skin, noting that although petroleum jelly is ideal for this purpose, most women do not like to use it because it feels tacky. Mineral oil, baby oil, cold cream, or water-continuous emulsions are acceptable substitutes.

Cosmetics help a woman, particularly in middle age, to highlight and brighten the latent colors in her skin tones and hair; of that there is no doubt. Forty is a good time to take a new look and a fresh approach to makeup. Try eyebrow pencil, shadow, eyeliner, powder bases, and new shades of lipstick and rouge. All women over forty must be prepared to devote more time to their makeup than they did at sixteen or even thirty. A young girl or woman can get away with only a few dabs of lipstick, but the older woman needs to learn the judicious use of moisturizer, base, rouge, powder, and eye makeup. To decide on the right colors, a visit to the five-and-ten-cent-store cosmetics counter is advisable; you can stock up on a variety of preparations with which to experiment without a large outlay of cash.

Many women wear too little makeup during the day and too much at night. Fluorescent lighting in offices and other places has made it necessary to use more color. Ethel Burge is bothered by the fact that mature women seem to avoid eye makeup. "They will wear lipstick but they are afraid to experiment with accentuating the eyes, and this is the most positive quality in the face," she says. Mrs. Burge, the author of *This Business of Dressing for*

Business, reports that when she urges women to wear eye makeup, they respond that they have no idea how to apply it or where to go for advice.

Whatever measures you take, you can't stop aging, warns Letitia Sage, senior associate editor of *Beauty Magazine*, but you can help the skin with a good, regular program of lubrication with night cream, provided it is not too oily. A dermatologist can advise about that and perhaps can recommend a good soap to use instead. If a husband objects to retiring with a greasy-faced wife, she can use a rich night cream while bathing or vacuuming and remove it later. Regular use of a moisturizer nurtures almost any skin, even an oily one. Going out with a protective moisturizing layer under your makeup, or even when you wear no makeup, helps to hold back the advancing years.

A STITCH IN TIME—PLASTIC SURGERY

With the medical and surgical advances that resulted largely from the development of plastic surgery in World War II, a woman does not have to surrender entirely to nature's attrition on face and figure. There was a time when people snickered about women who had had their faces lifted; no longer is it cause for levity, nor is it exclusively for film stars and the wealthy. The average patient is a middle-class housewife aged forty to sixty, according to Dr. Edgar P. Berry, chief of plastic surgery at Lenox Hill Hospital in New York. Women go to him and other surgeons for face-lifts to remove or minimize some of the telltale signs of aging—wrinkles, creases, pouches under the eyes, sagging jowls and eyelids, turkey-gobbler throats, loose upper arm skin, and overlarge or pendulous breasts. Plastic surgeons are also adept at peeling off layers of fat from abdomens, buttocks, thighs, and upper arms. As a matter of fact, there is scarcely an area that cannot be "lifted," and several theatrical and movie stars owe their perennially youthful appearances to the surgeon's scalpel.

If the goal is purely cosmetic and approached with a healthy attitude, surgeons provide their services, always with the warning that a new "you" will not emerge—only that you may possibly have a more youthful appearance. Responsible doctors are wary of those seeking to iron out psychological wrinkles as well as facial sags. A surgeon tries to make sure that a woman—or man—really wants the operation so she will look more like her old self and that she does not have hangups that will not be resolved through surgery.

A woman who thinks she might benefit from "having her face done" can get an idea of what the results might be by standing before a mirror and lifting the sagging skin with her hands. This gives an approximation of what an operation might accomplish—eliminating lines, deflating the bags around the eyes, minimizing jowls, and smoothing the neck.

No operation can be performed without leaving a scar; the trick is to try to place it where it will not be readily noticed. An incision is usually made behind the hairline, in the natural crease in front of the ear or behind it; it takes very close inspection to see most scars, and many, such as those around the eyes, disappear in two to four weeks. Moreover, the pain is minimal and is controlled with medication. Suntans are not advised, for they bring out any scars that would otherwise remain invisible except on the closest scrutiny.

"Most women leave town to have the operation," Dr. Berry said. "The change is not drastic, but they return looking better. The usual comment from friends is: 'My, you're looking well. Have you been south baking in the sun?' No doubt some friends are going to be suspicious, but plastic surgery is acceptable—particularly in this day and age."

With the secrecy lid off, more and more women are talking about their facial operations, though a number of prominent actresses and world-famous women have had several without making a public announcement—although one of them has gone so far as to publicize hospital visits for tooth extractions and other minor ailments—but others discuss it freely. One who was so pleased with the results that she announced them publicly was Phyllis Diller, the comedienne, who disclosed that she had invested $4,000 in having her face lifted and her nose remodeled.

Dr. Berry finds that a woman benefits from the operation for five to seven years and sometimes longer. "Don't forget," he admonished, "that after five years she has aged another five years since the operation. However, she will be that much ahead of the woman who didn't have the face-lift."

As for finding the right doctor, Berry said that there are well-trained, capable plastic surgeons in small communities as well as large ones. He advises a woman to ask her family doctor or dermatologist for suggestions or to check with the county medical society or a hospital in her area.

A note of caution is being added by most reputable professionals in the field of plastic surgery. This concerns the peeling process that is being widely advertised as a restorer of youthful skin. So many women—and men too—have been disfigured by this technique that we have become convinced it is a risky measure. We might consider having our faces lifted, but never peeled.

DOES SHE OR DOESN'T SHE?

The slogan "Does she or doesn't she?" has become famous in an advertisement for hair-coloring products. The matter of hair color is not a woman's best-kept secret, however. There is another beauty secret held closely by most women, who find it embarrassing to discuss and often go without the best solution for their problem. The subject is hirsuteness, or, more precisely, excessive facial hair. Many young women are troubled with unwanted hair on upper lips and chins, and large numbers of middle-aged women are especially plagued by it and resort to all kinds of measures, usually in secret. Some shave. Others tweeze or use depilatories. Too many have permanently scarred their faces by investing in home electrolysis kits. None of these measures provides the right answers. The only permanent and safe method is electrolysis performed by a trained and approved operator, a process that involves an electric needle that destroys the hair root. If a woman has been troubled with hair on her face for a long time and has removed it, it may take more than one prick of the needle to eliminate each hair. Although there is a slight amount of pain involved, it is fleeting, and the results are permanent.

Dermatologists are usually able to recommend electrologists for the cosmetic removal of hair. Moles and other skin blemishes are the province of the dermatologist himself, since there is a potential danger of a cancerous or precancerous condition.

Dr. Robert Greenblatt, in his work at the Medical College of Georgia, estimates that about 40 per cent of American white females develop some facial hair with menopause. He attributes some cases to emotional stress or distress or overwork, some to heredity, and some to hormonal disbalance. X-ray treatment and long confinement to a plaster cast can also stimulate the growth of superfluous hair.

THE GRAY DOESN'T HAVE TO TATTLE

Like other parts of the body, hair is affected by the aging process. Medical authorities continue to be baffled about what causes hair loss and balding. More women than is commonly suspected are troubled with baldness, and not all women lose hair merely because of aging, for heredity has a lot to do with it. In a family where men have a propensity for baldness, the women may also have a problem, which means that, contrary to popular belief, they do lose hair as they age. Their foreheads may recede or they may develop bald spots at the crown. Even with considerable balding, women, as a rule, still lose their hair in smaller quantities than men and not usually to the point of complete baldness. There is a problem around the time of menopause, which doctors suspect can also be attributed to hormonal imbalance.

Whatever the cause, the wig fad that developed in the 1960s, for men as well as women, has proved to be a godsend to those with thinning hair who want to do something about it. As in the case of face-lifting, women used to be secretive about wearing falls and switches, and even wigs, which in times past were so crudely made that they were difficult to hide, as was the case with the Widow Zander in the Andy Gump comic strip that most of today's middle-agers read when they were children. Some hairpieces have been known in the past as fronts, and women were indeed putting up false fronts if they wore them. Now, with wigmaking techniques so perfected that false hair can be attractive, women are making no secret about wearing wigs and can even be heard boasting of how many they have in colors and styles other than their own. They carry wig cases aboard airliners and ships with great aplomb and without trying to pretend they are something else.

Gray hair also accompanies aging; why, nobody knows, beyond the fact that a hair becomes white when the inner layer of the hair shaft no longer contains pigment. Hair does not change color overnight; it is a gradual process, although with some people it is faster and earlier than with others. People in their twenties have turned gray, and some as old as eighty or more have no gray hairs, or few. On rare occasions grayness results from disease or some other condition, but generally it is nothing to be upset about, particularly since the hair can be colored, tinted, or otherwise made to look attractive—or covered with a wig. And, indeed, many a head of gray hair needs no embellishment.

Whether it be a wig or your own, the attractiveness of your hair depends on styling and sheen, and keeping it clean contributes to the total effect. Some people think hair is damaged by frequent shampoos, but this is another old wives' tale. How often you lather your hair has nothing to do with its condition beyond making it more attractive. Brushing can bring a shine to it by evenly distributing the oil exuded by the scalp and helping prevent split, dry ends, but Vidal Sassoon, the hair stylist, maintains that brushing hair one hundred strokes at night is useful only if a woman wants to build her biceps; he insists that it can do nothing for the hair. Facial isometrics and massaging the scalp can do more, he says, for they loosen and invigorate the scalp.

Mr. Sassoon says that every mature woman *should* have beautiful hair after years of working with it, but unfortunately that is not always the case. Most people tend to learn with experience, but when it comes to personal grooming, too many women remain "illiterate" all their lives, he says. He takes particular issue with the use of lacquer to hold hair in place and teasing hair to make it look full. "Anything a man can't get his hands through has to be unsexy," he commented. "When you touch hair, if it's healthy, you want to touch it again."

As for rollers, he recommends instant divorce for husbands of women who wear them in public. "A woman sleeping in rollers every night has really got to be joking!"

DRESSING THE PART

While little girls have always liked to dress up in their mother's clothes, some mothers make the mistake of trying to live like their little girls, although youth is no longer as much a matter of years as a state of mind. Women today seem to feel younger than those of the same age a few years ago, but at the same time they need to be reminded that some youthful styles and colors are not for them.

We talked with a number of fashion experts in our search for advice to the woman in her second forty, and they all contributed their ideas and suggestions.

One of them, Nora Aponte, the Italian designer, thinks mature women should forget about dark, severe colors, pastels, and little flowers and pot sleeves, and go in for bright shades. "I think red looks much better on a mature woman than pink," she said. "So does a dashing green of a courageous shade, which indicates that she is mature."

Philippe Heim, the French designer, advises against following fashion leaders. Everyone has her own problem and her own way of living, and what she wears should be adapted to them, he said. Pants, he and others noted, are becoming to older women who cannot wear miniskirts; not only do they look elegant in pants, but younger and slimmer as well.

Simonetta agrees that pants and tunics are the answer

for many women over forty. "It's not the age that counts; it's the spirit," she said. "I've seen old people at eighteen and very young ones at seventy. It's what you have inside that is important. Of course, after forty you don't have the strength and resistance you had at twenty. That is a physical thing."

In designing clothes for some of the more mature fashion pacesetters such as the Duchess of Windsor, Merle Oberon, and the Ford women, Simonetta has found that they are never hesitant to adopt new fashions, although they are selective and have ideas of their own. She encounters no problems with people who are sure of themselves, only with shy women who want to be up to date but are afraid to be different.

"I recall," Simonetta said, "that at the beach last summer there were lots of charming, beautiful young girls, practically naked. A fig leaf. Three fig leaves. And then one day came a woman who was not so young. She was not so beautiful as these young kids, and she had on a one-piece bathing suit. All the men turned around and looked at her.

"Very often women reaching the age of forty take it upon themselves to decide that youth is finished for them and that the time has come to assume a conservative look, which results only too often in the matronly look," she continued. "Remember the famous saying that life begins at forty? Most women count age in years and with the mirror, not realizing that youth and chic have no age—they are something inside you—it is the spirit and not the physique that counts."

Rudi Gernreich, another designer who caters to the wealthy, objects to the prevalent "youth hangup." "If you really relax about your age and grow older gracefully, you look much younger. Middle age is the time to cover the body and to concentrate on it. As people grow older, the body becomes a private matter . . . and therefore the body should be hidden to public view and abstracted so as not to accentuate itself. The important thing is not to be self-conscious about aging." He added the observation that improvement of one's carriage and makeup can bring on "another loveliness that comes with maturity."

For an evening of bridge at home, Eve Stillman advocates jumpsuits and tunics for comfort and because such attire is more glamorous and even exciting than a traditional housecoat. Also, she observed, "it's a great prelude to bed." And when it comes to bed, she advised, wear something both becoming and contemporary, not a dowdy nightgown. "It gives you a marvelous feeling of spirit," she said. "I think women over forty find themselves. Life becomes deeper, more appreciated. You know what you like and how to enjoy it. This is the best time of your life!"

The Irish designer Clodagh Kennedy, like Simonetta, is convinced that "it's the spirit that counts." Any woman can manage to get by in an adaptation of any new look if she has something to begin with, she commented, but "she can't suddenly become a sexy blonde type if she was always the skinny dark type. Mama usually goes out and tries on a dress—not even a way-out dress—with the wrong heels, and the balance gets upset, and she says she looks ridiculous and she can't wear it."

That, in Miss Kennedy's view, is approaching the problem from the wrong angle. Begin by buying a good pair of shoes, she advised, and get a new hairdo. File off long, pointed fingernails and trade in your old-fashioned girdle for pantyhose. Now you are ready to shop for something you really want to wear, but set out with the awareness that shopping is not what it used to be. Many things have changed in addition to the styles.

THE NEW LOOK IN SHOPPING

As an interesting side effect of the massive national diet kick, larger-size dresses are being eliminated from the more stylish lines of clothes. There are not as many large women as there were, and many departments specializing in half sizes have been phased out. The trend has been for women to get their figures into some kind of shape, with the result that sizes 18 and 20 are available in fashionable clothes in only limited supply.

Myra Rein, who specializes in boutique clothes, points out also that what used to be called cocktail dresses are as passé as the tea dance. Designers are making clothes in terms of size rather than age or occasion. What can a size 6 wear? What can a size 8 wear? Because women of all ages are interested in keeping their figures in check, many of the over-forty shoppers find themselves buying in the teen department.

One does not think of a labor union as an authority on fashion, but the International Ladies Garment Workers Union is an exception. The organization's Union Label Department has organized a Consumer Service Division, which has issued a booklet, *Looking Your Fashionable Age,* saying that "nobody looks at your age—only at you." And it added that "good fashion doesn't belong to the young, any more than green to spring or white to summer," so you should think of clothes in terms of your shape and type rather than your age.

When shopping, the union advisers suggest, regard yourself as someone special. Give everything you own and buy a second thought. If a dress, coat, suit, or blouse has something in common with something you already have, like, and look well in, you are building a wardrobe that looks like you. Study yourself in a mirror before buying a coat. If it fits at the shoulders, it will be all right all over. Sit down while trying on a coat or a dress, searching for bulges and strains, a neckline that chokes, a skirt that pulls, armholes that pinch. Keep your stomach tucked in, even if you are trying on a dress that has no waistline, for you may want to wear a belt with it.

One further word of advice from the union: if you have beautiful legs, and you are forty-five, show them. If you have fat, broad feet, wear a closed shoe. Regardless of what a woman wears, she should walk with her head high and shoulders back. The beach is a good place to take a walking "test." You walk properly if you can step through sand barefoot without becoming tired.

Ethel Burge, speaking as a lecturer, consultant, and fashion-show coordinator, gave us some additional guidelines to pass along for those interested in self-examination in buying clothes.

1. A short neck calls for flat, narrow lapels on suits and dresses and necklines cut into a V, as low as is deemed proper. Brimless hats are good, if one still feels that hats are necessary, and roll-back collars are good.

2. Shop only when you are in the mood, for spontaneity helps in choosing clothes.

3. Heavy women should beware of skirts that are too short.

There are some designers who create clothes with the mature woman in mind. Jo Copeland is one of these, according to Mrs. Burge, although most of her colleagues have only the young, perfect figure in mind, which is "rather alarming to those of us who have figure imperfections." But, Mrs. Burge said, "it's a challenge in a way, too, to find ways of converting the best of fashion into your own thing. The key is to find what is right for *you.*"

It is Mrs. Burge's theory that the middle-aged women who wears the wrong clothes probably has never been much interested in fashions or how she looks. There is nothing the matter with that; she is interested in something else that is more important to her. But it *can* be unfortunate, for as Mrs. Burge says, "dressing attractively is really the first requisite of success in anything that you are doing. You don't have to be consumed with interest in fashion to look well, but it is important, and people react more favorably to you if you dress as well as you can.

"However," she commented, "most of the women who have done the wrong things are not aware of it. They are happy with themselves. If they are holding down good jobs, and if their husbands are happy with them and their bosses are happy with them, who is to say, 'Look, you need a renovation'? So I never do."

Periodically, our figures undergo slight changes, which mean that we should adapt our clothes to these changes as well as to our changing life-styles. A woman can look ridiculous in the same kind of dresses that became her at eighteen. That does not mean she should wear matronly-looking attire, but she should make every effort to select styles that are becoming to her *now* and that are useful in her daily activities.

It helps if a woman can find someone she trusts, on whose judgment she relies, to help her look at herself with a critical eye and make suggestions. Seldom can we take the opinion of a saleswoman, who has more interest in the sound of the cash register than in how we look, and it is impossible for us to see ourselves as others do.

If help is not available, then there are ways to make judgments for oneself. Pauline Trigère counsels that women should forget about their age and look for what they like and what they look well in. When buying a dress, she says, always take a good look from the back and sides as well as the front, and remember that the model who looked marvelous in the dress when it was advertised is long and lean—and the cameraman was kind to her. Few paying customers can ever look as well turned out.

AFTER THE MIRROR, WHAT?

Suppose a woman has done all—or at least some—of the things we have suggested to keep in trim and look attractive in her clothes. Now she opens her mouth to speak and blows the whole scene in one sentence. Only now does she realize that her voice can age along with the rest of her and be a dead giveaway that she is getting on in years. She may not be about to croak, although she can sound as though she is.

Just as the body ages, so does the voice; and, likewise, some voices, like some bodies, age more rapidly than others. If a woman keeps her body in good shape through exercise and diet, she should be interested in keeping her voice from deteriorating too. It helps a lot to preserve the vocal image of youth with the same diligence one gives to work on figure, hair, skin, makeup, and clothes.

Dorothy Uris, a voice and speech consultant who formerly played in motion pictures as Dorothy Tree, says that correct use of the voice provides the best way to preserve its youthful verve. She recommends reading aloud and even talking into a tape recorder. The person who reads with ease and pauses in the right places will find, on playing her voice back, that it sounds unlike the voice she uses in conversation or on the telephone. What she needs to do is to close the gap between her daily speaking voice and her recording voice in an effort to achieve consistency. Those who have a difficult time might benefit from a visit to a speech therapist.

"Little girls should be seen and not heard was a popular adage in my day," Mrs. Uris said. "I don't know whether or not it is still said to little girls, but it's a bad thing to say. It has produced a voice that's practically inaudible. Women think this is feminine but it reflects lack of communication of their identification as equal citizens in our society. It causes them to take a backward role."

Clear speech and a pleasant tone of voice are social assets that reflect an outgoing personality. Women often tend to develop voice styles that either they or someone else thinks fit their personalities. For example, Mrs. Uris cited a woman who, though mature, thought of herself as a doll, something cute and bright, and adopted a style of speaking that reflected this self-image. Many women she has encountered speak in the voice they think a man wants to hear—a childish, high-pitched tone, the Marilyn Monroe whisper, or the smoky huskiness of the café singer. This is playacting, in Mrs. Uris's book, and not nearly so attractive as the voice that communicates readily; is free of nasality, rasps, lisps, and other affectations; and is soft but firm and certainly not shrill.

"In this day of the women's liberation movement," she remarked, "women have to liberate their voices too along with their minds and their professions. They must match their voices to their opportunities. The voice a woman presents in her role as a woman, in her career, in her life's work is as much a part of her personality as any other factor."

It is never too late to work on one's voice, just as it is never too late to lose weight, get rid of the flab, change hairdos, and learn new makeup techniques. Getting involved in updating one's exterior is part of getting through the middle-age era of patch and repair, through which we all must eventually go, if we live long enough.

CHAPTER 5

Tuning In on Marriage and Family Life

MIDDLE AGE IS a time of great challenges and opportunities. It also has its pitfalls, for it is a time in which a women can be caught in the middle in more ways than one. Not only is she at a crossroads in her own life. She may also be caught up in the lives of others, finding herself in the midst of a two-way generation gap. On one side of the chasm, she is confronted by her aging parents, who, in a sense, are becoming *her* children. On the other, she is faced with her own children, who are young adults or are moving toward maturity. She may have trouble communicating with both.

Added to this is the possibility of another kind of breach, one that often develops between husbands and wives in middle age. After twenty or twenty-five years of marriage, it sometimes is not as easy for them to communicate as it was during the early years. Money and its relation to old-age security becomes an issue. The onset of menopause can pose problems, as we have seen. A man's career frustrations and the prospect of retirement become unsettling to him and the rest of the family. In other words, a family evolves along with its life-style and with the changes that take place in its members, and new lines of communication are sometimes needed.

A never-ending stream of so-called expertise pours forth about troubled American families. *Is marriage in trouble?* asks a magazine article on the high divorce rate. *Is the family obsolete?* asks another describing how members of countless families are going their separate ways. And, finally, we have *The American family: Is its future uncertain?* A proliferation of articles delve into the youth rebellion, the women's liberation movement, communal living, increased mobility, and the economic and social pressures that are causing anthropologists such as Margaret Mead to ask "Can the family survive?" Without the family unit, our society faces extinction, declares Dr. Paul Popenoe, the psychologist; while Morton Hunt, a writer specializing in sociological matters, puts it another way: "Marriage is not going to expire soon unless civilization itself expires or mankind exterminates himself."

Such questions and declarations may sell magazines, but are they producing the right answers for worried, harassed readers? When did you last read an article stating the positive view that while it *is* true that one out of every four American marriages ends in the failure spelled d-i-v-o-r-c-e, the three others have endured? Most couples who marry find ways to make the grade somehow, but who gives us reassurance as we muddle through our lives?

Morton Hunt is far less pessimistic than some, concluding that what may appear to be signs of the disintegration of modern marriage are actually indications of adaptation and experimentation in survival. He points out that those who divorce and remarry two, three, or even four times —what some call "serial polygamy"—are adjusting their lives to the ethics of a monogamous society to "fit emotional realities and the long life expectancy of today."

While fundamental concepts of marital life continue to evolve, most of us go along on a day-to-day basis working with our own family relations on all levels—psychological, economic, and social. That we are managing well is confirmed by information such as the estimate made in 1971 that two million post-World War II couples, most of them now in their forties, were about to observe their silver wedding anniversaries. That so many remained together in the face of dynamic economic and social change is a tribute to all, but we sometimes wonder whether, in some respects, the balance of credit should not weigh more heavily on the side of the wife.

It may be that the world of the mature married woman has changed more during her lifetime than has that of her husband. True, changes have swept business, industry, and the professions, but what could be a longer trip for a woman than the one that has taken her out of the role of scullery maid, baby-sitter, laundress, housekeeper, full-time cook, and furnace attendant and made her a push-button home executive who, while she may devote considerable time to keeping house, is freed from most of the drudgery. Her world has changed during her lifetime from one of hanging the card out for the iceman and rushing to get ice cream home from the drugstore in the hope it would not melt before dessert to reaching into the deep freeze for ice cubes and ice cream whenever they are needed.

These are obvious examples of how life has improved for the American woman; what they spell is unbelievable progress. The grandmother of one of the authors made her first journey in a covered wagon and her last by jet airplane. Her first meal as a bride was cooked on a wood stove; she had no telephone, electricity, or running water. During her lifetime came electrification of homes and factories; invention of the telephone, radio, and television; manufacture of the first motor cars and airplanes;

and the transition from wood to coal oil to gas to electric stoves, from the galvanized tub and corrugated washboard to mechanical washer-driers, from coal furnaces to oil burners and heat by electricity and gas. All these developments, many of them in relatively recent years, have revolutionized American life in general and have given us a higher standard of living than any other country.

Along with the material advances have come changes in the entire lives of women—their work and sex lives, their child-rearing techniques, and their attitudes and behavior. As children, most of us probably lived near grandparents, uncles, aunts, and cousins who were always there when they were needed. Young mothers in those days had the security of relatives living nearby, while today families may be separated by thousands of miles. A mother must learn to solve her own problems, as well as those of her husband and children, without being able to lean on the shoulder of wiser older relatives.

In middle age, especially, a woman may need help with a whole new set of problems that older women already have lived through. Dr. Catherine S. Chilman, dean of the faculty of Hood College, in Frederick, Maryland, has drawn up a list of some of the important concerns families have in the midstage of their development. Dr. Chilman, formerly a member of the staff of the Department of Health, Education, and Welfare, cites these as a sample: the emotional upheaval of raising adolescent children, which can tear parents apart; extramarital affairs, particularly among husbands of the middle and upper classes; occupational restlessness that engulfs some men when they realize that their boyhood dreams have not been fulfilled; family expenses, which peak in the parents' middle years, largely because of college costs; the possibility that older parents may become either financially or physically dependent on their middle-aged children.

These typify the crises that are most likely to rock us in the "stormy forties." If couples can weather that decade, they have reason to hope for calm after the storm. In the meantime, a woman must work constantly at adjusting to new roles within her family, such as becoming a mother-in-law and a grandmother. She finds herself learning to mother her own parents without the aid of guidance by a gerontological Dr. Spock, and she must develop a deeper understanding of her husband and his problems as he grows older and possibly increasingly frustrated in his workaday life.

Weathering the storms is part of living and growing, and couples who "make it" have strong chances of celebrating their golden wedding anniversaries together. In getting through middle age, however, a woman has to work at preserving her marriage, maintaining her health, retaining her sense of humor, and developing a deeper understanding of others, while at the same time finding ways to generate energy and good cheer throughout the family. Most important is her effort to encourage warmth and affection from her husband for herself and the rest of the family.

PUTTING MARITAL COMMUNICATIONS ON THE RIGHT WAVELENGTH

A fifty-year-old woman telephoned her husband at his office and asked for an appointment to see him.

"What in the world for?" he demanded.

"Because I want to talk to you," she responded.

"But, darling, can't we talk at home tonight?" he persisted.

"No," she declared. "When you are at home you talk *at* me, not to me or with me, and you don't really listen to what I have to say. I have some ideas I want to talk over with you, and I decided that your office was the only place I could get your undivided attention."

Not many wives, especially one who has been married for thirty years, would go to such lengths to get a word in edgewise, but communications problems persist in many a marriage. Attorneys and marriage counselors listen to constant complaints about barriers between married couples, particularly after twenty or thirty years of sharing the same bed and board but seldom exchanging confidences.

"He doesn't understand me," the wife complains.

"She doesn't listen to me," the husband retorts.

Breakdowns in communications have become the number-one problem of couples who have been married for many years, according to Dr. Mary Jane Hungerford, a counselor affiliated with the American Institute of Family Relations. She offered a few suggestions to help marital partners who no longer seem to be on the same wavelength. One remedy she recommends is that a husband and wife who feel they are out of touch should set aside a specific time every evening—perhaps only ten or fifteen minutes—in which to drop whatever they are doing and sit down and talk with each other—and listen. Sometimes this works better if each has his own say on alternate evenings, with the husband airing his views one night and his wife the next. When it is the husband's turn to take the floor, the wife must be ready "to absorb what he is dishing out," Dr. Hungerford says. After a couple have followed this procedure for a while, the communications lines are bound to be open again; husband and wife should be back in touch and hearing one another as clearly as ever.

Counselors have developed a variety of communications gimmicks that they recommend to their clients, including "no interruptions" and "checking back." The ground rules for these techniques provide that if one person is speaking, the other must let him finish without interrupting. The listener then checks back, summarizing what he has heard to make sure the point was made clearly—and understood.

"Communication," explains Dr. Hungerford, "is not just what we ourselves broadcast, but learning to receive the broadcast of the other person and checking back on what you think you've received. The key is recognition that the only authority on what is meant by any statement is the person who said it in the first place."

In addition to using these techniques, an "old married" couple might consider taking a tip that is often given to young people in premarital counseling sessions. They are advised to take an inventory on their first anniversary to determine how well their union is working out and to make the necessary adjustments. Such a tuning-up session calls for a frank discussion of sexual adjustments or hang-ups, finances, any nettlesome differences in temperament, relations with parents and in-laws, the direction they are going socially and recreationally, and the emerging style of their family life. Of great importance is their need to discuss how they are communicating and to air any complaints as frankly and dispassionately as possible.

As we thought about this, it became clear to us that there should be no reason why a couple should go through this procedure only once, after the first year of marriage. Why not take stock on every anniversary? It may be more important for couples who have been married twenty years or more to have an annual inventory than it is for the newly married. In any case, more than an encounter is called for. After the points of contention or dissatisfaction are laid bare, they should be acted upon through appropriate changes in family relationships or altered life-styles or habits.

Unfortunately, many people enter marriage thinking they are going to be able to "reform" or change their partner rather than being willing to accept him as he is.

One frustration that emerges after years of marriage is disappointment because the hoped-for changes have not occurred. A number of marriages founder on this point.

A study of some 2,500 married people designed to discover what made some happy and others miserable found that the couples who seemed most happily married were those who could say things such as, "We are good companions and have very few conflicts"; "We always resolve our disagreements by mutual adjustment"; "We find little or nothing in marriage to complain of"; "We don't regret the choice we made, and we would choose each other again"; "We consider our marriage to be definitely happier than the average." How many couples can make any of those points or are willing to discuss them openly?

Holding successful "open forums" within the family depends in large part on selection of the right time and place. Some couples find they communicate best in bed, after the lights have been turned off, when they are relaxed and comfortable. Others are too fatigued, and therefore are likely to be too crabby, to think clearly about problems at bedtime, so perhaps a chat over morning coffee would be more appropriate. Regardless of the time, a couple who really want to get down to essentials will not engage in their frank exchanges in front of their children, relatives, or friends. Not only would this tend to be inhibiting but it might also prove to be embarrassing.

Ideally, of course, no couple should have to resort to the artifices of scheduled conferences or presenting "agendas" of grievances. A truly well adjusted husband and wife will have time for each other whenever it is sought. They should be able to communicate openly and freely at any time; but for the many who have been reluctant to "call a spade a spade" and have been plunged into married misery, a prescribed program can be helpful. One thing seems certain: if the partners have not communicated openly in the early days of their marriage, each passing year will have made it more difficult for them to break the silence. If that becomes the case, a visit to a marriage counselor or a family-service agency—and as soon as possible before matters become even worse—may be in order.

THE ART OF FAMILY FIGHTING

Show us a couple who claim they have never had a quarrel or disagreement, and you are pointing to two people who do not really care very deeply about one another. Healthy differences of opinion are indications of a healthy marriage, in which both parties feel secure enough in their love to risk setting off fireworks periodically. We are not talking about the constantly battling family, but rather about the man and woman who are concerned enough about one another to point out shortcomings, mistakes, and areas of improvement.

Some psychotherapists maintain that hidden anger can burst like a volcano at any time and wreck a marriage. There are those who go so far as to recommend "fight clinics" where marital spats can be controlled by a third party who is an expert in these matters. "A healthy expression of aggression is just another form of love, rather than the traditional romantic notion that anger and aggression and conflict are symptoms of a deterioration of a relationship," says Dr. George S. Bach, director of the Institute of Group Psychotherapy in Beverly Hills, California, and coauthor of *The Intimate Enemy*.

He believes that because there is a basic power conflict between two intimate individuals, they should be taught how to bring out their differences in an open fight. The more mature and individualistic a person is, the more likely he is to have his own way of doing things. If the differences between him and his mate are suppressed, they can fester and cause open wounds.

"Older couples tend to be more patient than younger

ones," Dr. Bach maintains. "They are more aware that marriage is really a challenge rather than something to be taken for granted. They tend to be more realistic. They have given up the romantic dreams. On the other hand, the older group is handicapped (compared to younger ones) in their pessimism and conservatism about what can be done about certain realities of marriage. The younger ones are willing to try the fight techniques; the older ones have more rituals to overcome because they have lived together longer and their list of hurts is longer and their 'gunnysack of injustice' is fuller."

Here are some of the rules for constructive argument advocated by Dr. Bach and his associates:

1. Once an argument is over, forget it. Don't hark back to it the next time you fight.

2. Try to arrive at an understanding of what the issue really is. Sometimes a deep-seated grievance is masked as a petty annoyance.

3. Don't insist on winning an argument with an open admission by your adversary that you were in the right.

It is Dr. Bach's conviction that the only successful family quarrels are those that end in a draw; both partners should feel they have won before a genuine truce can be achieved. If either is made to appear the loser, the fight not only has gone nowhere but can be destructive.

MONEY AS A SOURCE OF FRICTION

What do families most frequently fight about? *Money.* We know a couple whose regular battles echo through the hall on a high floor of an expensive apartment house, and the subject is invariably money—the spending of it. These are well-to-do people on the brink of retirement who, in their decades together, have been unable to discuss finances without an explosion. Yet they, unlike many other couples who bicker about money, have remained together—miserable, yet together. Ruth Horowitz, a Summit, New Jersey, marriage counselor, finds that such squabbles over finances are a common cause of separation and divorce, largely because money has a deep emotional value, rooted principally in security, or the lack of it. "Some people feel it gives them status, prestige, and power," she says, "but at its deepest level, money really stands for love. When somebody spends money on others or on themselves, they feel they are loved."

A woman may buy an expensive hat or exotic perfume to convince herself that she is loved. A man may gamble or bet on the horses as a display of his feelings of disdain toward the person he loves. The misuse of money or unwarranted extravagance by either spouse can make the other feel threatened. Like so many other problems in marriage, money is tied to the role each plays. As the years pass and a couple learns to arrive at some understanding of the mechanics of day-to-day management of money, the emphasis gradually shifts from budgeting and the extras of life to what money represents in their lives—most often security. With more wives working to provide a second income and more husbands helping with the housework, the attitudes of both toward money also change.

Norman Lobsenz, coauthor of *How to Stay Married*, who has worked closely with the Family Service Association in studying the role of money in marriage, believes that "at any stage of marriage, you always carry with you an attitude toward money which, by and large, is inherited from your parents' attitude toward it. A woman who grew up in a household which was concerned with money, where money was saved for that rainy day in the future which might never come, is going to be quite concerned if her husband says, 'O.K., now let's go around the world.' It's a very difficult thing to accept that you are approaching your mature years and therefore you still think you must save for that rainy day and your old age."

He also points out that arguments about money, like sex, are often not really at the root of the problem. Because it is not socially acceptable for people to debate about their basic psychological views of life—if, indeed, they are aware of them at all—money becomes a kind of whipping boy through which they can either get rid of the anxieties and conflicts they have harbored all their lives or intensify them.

If more couples were to realize that their overt money problems are actually based on their attitudes toward money and the emotions about money that are aroused in them, rather than the actual dollars and cents, they might be able to take a more realistic approach in revising their budgets—and their attitudes—as they grow older. Such an awakening might enable them to discard their now-outdated ideas of what money represents and which member of the family is best equipped to handle it. They might even consider abandoning the his and hers bank accounts that strain many marriages and pooling their resources.

ACCEPTING FINANCIAL RESPONSIBILITY

Every woman, whether she goes to work or toils at home, should be equipped to assume part of the financial responsibility for herself and her family. She should gain an understanding of how to budget according to income, how much to invest and how much to save, how to manage mortgage payments, how to get the most out of insurance policies, how to approach drawing a will, and how to deal with installment buying and credit. "A woman can evaluate her own worth by knowing exactly what is coming in and exactly what is going out for the same period," declared the late Faye Henle, a money-management expert. "If she can watch where it goes, she can control a lot of money."

Just as couples should periodically check up on their personal relationship, they might also consider holding quarterly meetings of their family board of directors to appraise their financial situation. Is their income keeping pace with their cost of living? Are their debts manageable? Are they facing any major expenses they cannot meet? Do they have a savings program for the future?

In preparing a quarterly family report, you should draw a balance sheet showing your net worth. List all your assets and liabilities; total the two columns and then subtract the liabilities from the assets to determine what you are worth (if your liabilities exceed your assets, you are in trouble).

Assets consist of money in checking and savings accounts, as well as the market value of securities and the cash value of insurance, annuities, real estate, personal property such as automobiles, furniture, furs, jewelry, etc., and any other items such as personal loans due you. Your liabilities include the mortgage, installment debts, accounts payable for household bills, and other obligations such as current taxes.

Now that you know what you are worth, study your cash flow to see where the money goes. How much comes in regularly in salaries, bonuses, loans, interest and dividends, tax refunds, gifts, etc.? What goes out in mortage or rent payments, installment buying, insurance premiums, taxes, savings, food, household costs, transportation, clothing, car maintenance, and recreation? This should put the finishing touches on your financial picture.

INSURANCE AS A HEDGE AGAINST THE FUTURE

Most adults have some kind of insurance, whether it be group, major medical, and Blue Cross policies, an individual life or accident policy, or an annuity with a life clause.

Have you read your policies lately—if ever? Do you know what your coverage really is? Do you know the difference between cash-value policies, term policies, and annuities? Can you borrow money on your policy? Have you reviewed your coverage to determine if you need to update it? If you are past forty and have no children or anyone else for whom you want to build an estate, do you really need life insurance? Perhaps it could be converted to an annuity providing regular payments or a lump-sum settlement on retirement. Health insurance is a must for those forty to sixty-five, when Medicare takes over, at least in part; but as Miss Henle said, "There's no way of telling anyone how much health insurance to have." Everyone must figure this out for himself.

When it comes to life insurance, the Institute of Life Insurance reported that about 14 per cent of the life policies in force in the United States in 1970—more than $200 billion in face value—covered women. In addition, women are the major beneficiaries of life insurance, receiving about two-thirds of the payments. Nearly 75 per cent of adult women own some form of life coverage; however, the face value is far less than that of policies taken out on the lives of men.

WHEN HELP IS NEEDED—MARRIAGE COUNSELING

By bumbling through, many families seem to be able to cope with their financial problems, and other difficulties, year in and year out without seeking special guidance or counsel; their instincts, childhood training, and sometimes just sheer luck seem to help them over the hurdles. But increasing numbers of people are finding that emotional problems or misunderstandings have snowballed to such an extent that they simply cannot see beyond them. It is at this point that a couple might consider taking their problems to a marriage counselor; there are many good ones, well trained and certified.

An understandable reluctance keeps many people from looking for such help because they are ashamed to admit that they have not been able to make it on their own. However, it is no more disgraceful to consult a marriage counselor about a marriage headed for the rocks than it is to go to a doctor with a fractured bone.

A study made by the National Institute of Mental Health some years ago showed that most people who want help with their psychological problems go to their clergyman first. Much of the marriage counseling now available is provided in the studies of a large proportion of the nation's 250,000 clergymen. Seminaries have added courses in psychological counseling to their curriculums, and there are several training centers for clergymen, the largest and oldest being the American Foundation of Religion and Psychiatry in New York, which turns out highly skilled pastoral counselors, many of them expert in marriage problems.

Whether a clergyman or a layman, the marriage counselor serves as a catalyst who can stand at the center of the marriage and look at it objectively before suggesting ways to break the deadlock. Admittedly there are marriages that cannot and should not continue, but Dr. Popenoe of the American Institute of Family Relations is one of those who takes the view that at least half the people who go their separate ways would probably have been better off if they could have found the right advice and straightened out their lives together.

For those who need help, the Family Service Association is an excellent referral agency, as are the American Association of Marriage and Family Counselors, 6303 Lemmon Avenue, Dallas, Texas 75209, and the American Association of Pastoral Counselors, 31 West 10th Street, New York, New York 10011. Any local or state mental health society can suggest reputable counselors.

Others—psychologists, social workers, doctors, and lawyers—offer counseling in conjunction with their work. Many marriage counselors listed in the Yellow Pages of the telephone book are engaged in other professions, serving as counselors on the side. A number of them are qualified; some are not. Unfortunately, many quacks, charlatans, and pseudopsychologists have invaded the field because only three states—California, Michigan, and New Jersey—regulate marriage counseling. Elsewhere, anyone who wants to be a marriage counselor can hang out a shingle and advertise his availability. Because of this, the American Association of Marriage and Family Counselors has begun a crusade to persuade all states to establish licensing regulations.

Despite the phony psychologists many marriages trip over, thousands of couples have successfully sought professional help in gluing together their disintegrating lives. Where there are no counselors—and most of them are concentrated in a few large states, mainly in major cities—couples might engage in self-examination in which they periodically check out their marriages, as we suggested earlier in this chapter.

"Put yourself in your mate's shoes," one counselor advises. "Try to feel what life feels like to him. Ask yourself, what does he need from me? How can I help make his life better and meet his needs? You'll find he's going to reciprocate by looking at *your* needs and trying to make your life better, too."

PLANNING AHEAD—
THE 150TH WEDDING ANNIVERSARY

Some day, scientists believe, it may be possible to prolong human life to the seemingly incredible age of 150 or 175 years through the perfection of artificial organ and transplant operations. Should this occur, one can foresee couples celebrating their 125th or 150th wedding anniversaries. When you consider the problems some families encounter in only twenty years together, it numbs the imagination to contemplate what their marriages might be like through a century.

The more conservative estimates are that by the end of this century the average life-span may be extended by ten to twenty years. One of those who contemplates this is Dr. Roderic Gorney, a psychiatrist, director of the program on Psychosocial Adaptation and the Future at the UCLA School of Medicine and author of *The Human Agenda.* Dr. Gorney sees no reason why continued improvement in medicine and public health cannot enable the average person to live to eighty, ninety, and even one hundred years of age.

With all the talk about longevity, medical science has not yet proposed ways to improve the quality as well as the quantity of life so that people can really enjoy their added years. In the context of this discussion, we wonder if they have given any thought to what will happen to marriage. Can an individual—*any* individual—remain married to the same person for 100, 125, or 150 years? Or would divorce become the order of the day for the new Methuselahs? As has been noted, the largest number of divorces involve those over forty-five who succumb to the "twenty-year slump." With greatly increased longevity, we wonder whether there might not be forty-, sixty-, and perhaps even eighty-year slumps as well. Imagine a girl marrying in her late teens, divorcing in her late twenties to marry again, and repeating this procedure periodically.

"Human beings at different epochs of their lives may really require something different in the way of marital relationship," Dr. Gorney comments. "Of course, the hope is that really mature personalities will be able to find someone with whom all those epochs of life could be lived through with each changing sufficiently so that they can meet the needs of the other person. But if that proves not to be the case in a particular instance, it seems to me that one of the changes that is going on and will become increasingly obvious is that people will accept a series of marital partnerships that match the needs of different parts of the life span."

Our traditional view of monogamy—being married to the same person "until death do us part"—may have to yield with biological change, but psychologically it has a valuable stabilizing role in our society. "The survival benefits of love," says Dr. Gorney, "have to do with giving the individual a sense of his own identity and validation of his existence and worth. And those things are likely to remain very significant to human beings for a long time. They need not necessarily, of course, be transferred in the relationship between one man and one woman, but that happens to be a very common and likely pattern for the future."

WHAT IS REALLY BUGGING MOM AND DAD

Adolescence, with its growing pains, sexual development, and educational demands is considered the most difficult single period of life, and it may be almost as traumatic for parents as it is for their children. In many families youngsters are going through puberty as Mom endures the monopause and Dad encounters his own physiological, psychological, and career changes. The concerns of parents about their children are heightened by their anxieties about themselves. A mother may be in the midst of her fifth hot flash of the day when her daughter rushes to tell her that she thinks she is menstruating for the first time; both are so wrapped up in what is going on inside them at that moment that they may fail to communicate adequately.

A subconscious jealousy of a daughter who is just embarking on the most fulfilling years of her life may be harbored by a mother who is terrified lest her desirability be at an end. The mother-daughter conflicts that ensue can be charged with dynamite. Dr. Chilman says that the "mood swings" caused by menopause in the mother and menstruation in the daughter involve "nearly identical anxieties about sexual adequacy and functioning, about forbidden sexual desires and fantasies." Mother and daughter can only vaguely communicate about these matters, so the mother may react to the situation by becoming overly restrictive about her daughter's social life or forbidding the use of makeup or otherwise trying to keep her a little girl. Quarrels over dating hours, studies, and all manner of trivia may ensue, with both becoming involved in the extremes of what has come to be known as the generation gap.

While the daughter may turn to her father because of her hostility toward her mother and her natural inclination toward the opposite sex, a son may now become disdainful of his father and seek deeper communication with his mother, as a woman. The teens are the period when boys and girls begin to think their parents are pretty dumb—not "with it." One young man of our acquaintance even went so far as to inform his father that he was a failure for not having been more of a success than he already was. Such verbal onslaughts would be easier to take if Dad were younger, but he has plunged into middle age plagued by feelings of uncertainty; a few unkind words from his son are all he needs to sap his morale even more. The result? Father and son stop communicating. They, too, are parties to the generation gap.

While the parents may be licking their wounds, they also are deeply aware that adolescence can be very difficult. A majority of the middle-aged women questioned by the Langley Porter Neuropsychiatric Institute attested to this, agreeing that the teens are the worst period of life.

The researchers who analyzed the findings concluded that the women were talking about their children, not their own adolescences. They clearly perceived the struggle through physical growth and interpersonal and heterosexual relations, the desire for independence, and the search for identity, all of which place a terrific strain on family life.

The adolescent, struggling to separate from the family and achieve some degree of independence, is growing increasingly competent intellectually, creatively, physically, and socially. His behavior may become confused and even erratic, with the parents making the mistake of associating it with "difficult" behavior of earlier years and interpreting it as retrogression rather than growth. They become convinced that the family as a unit is deteriorating.

Not only are the parents uptight about their own biological problems at this time, but they may be concerned about current family expenses as well as retirement, as we have noted. The father may feel trapped in his job because of his responsibilities at home. He may resent the fact that his wife is so deeply involved in their children's emotional turmoil that he has been made to feel as though he was taking second place. The marital friction that results may send either parent, or both, to the children for emotional support, thus polarizing the family.

The generation gap may be widened by an unnecessary and unwarranted concern by parents that their children might bring dishonor on the family name. Parents contribute to widening the gap through misunderstanding or pure selfishness. Still other causes for the breach between generations have been found by Dr. Clark E. Vincent of the Behavioral Sciences Center at the Bowman Gray School of Medicine, Wake Forest University, who attributes some of the trouble to fads in child-rearing theories and practices. From 1920 to 1935, he notes, the "parents' era" held sway; this emphasized a mother's competence and right to decide what her children's *needs* were and when and how they were to be met. The next major fad, from 1945 to 1960, known as the "children's era," saw the fusion of "wants" and "needs." In other words, what a child wanted was presumed, even by nutritionists, to be needed, and therefore had to be provided.

The middle-aged parents of today's teen-agers not only were reared in the era of restrictive parents but also were influenced by the Great Depression of the 1930s and the work ethic of the period. Their children are products of the permissive era and prosperity, and so are accustomed to having their wants regarded as their needs; they are the Now Generation—"I want it *now!*"

Heaped on this disparity is the burden of guilt saddling a large proportion of parents who assume too much credit —and therefore too much blame—for their influence on their children. There is a tendency on the part of a significant segment of parents in the thirty-five-to-fifty-five age-group to see themselves as failures as parents when they are confronted by teenagers who insist on rights that seem extraordinary, special privileges, and permissive behavior. The sense of parental failure that results, according to Dr. Vincent, often exacts a price from mothers who respond to the pressures by developing symptoms and ailments that defy treatment.

It would be possible for parents and teen-agers to live more harmoniously if the parents tried to gain an understanding of the gap between them. They might benefit from knowing, for example, that boys and girls are maturing earlier than in the past and that the age level is dropping every year, as concluded by an exhaustive study of human growth involving thousands of girls, four generations of Harvard students, and other research. An accompanying acceleration in mental development has been detected, which scientists feel could have wide social and legal implications if it can be confirmed. Earlier intellectual and physical maturity call for more help than ever for the teen-ager.

Adults in their middle years are, on the average, still on a far higher emotional plane than their teen-agers. They should by now have established a philosophical track on which to run, and they also have the fruits of their experience in the community, in work, and in their relationships with each other. Although they may be in the throes of a middle-aged psychological upheaval, it should be only temporary, just as the pangs of adolescence eventually subside.

"The generation gap exists only where parents are unwilling to accept the disparity in maturity that exists between them and their children and to make peace with it," writes Dr. Bruno Bettleheim in the *Ladies' Home Journal.* "Parents and children cannot even be friends, because friendship presupposes not only equality but also independence from each other. Closeness need not mean equality. We can take what they say and do very seriously without being bowed over by it, and we don't have to doubt our own values because our children don't like them."

AFTER ADOLESCENCE, WHAT?

Most families seem to survive the children's adolescence. Then a new kind of crisis develops; the youngsters go off to college, never to return, or move away from home to live and work on their own, or get married and establish their own families. This puts a great strain on a marriage, second only to the birth of the first child. The mother may feel abandoned. The father feels he has lost his "moonlighting" job as a parent, but he still has his work to keep him occupied, while his wife finds she is "unemployed" and time is hanging heavy.

For the woman whose life has not revolved around the home—the career woman or community worker—the blow is not so severe. But the mother who has centered her life on her home and children is frequently devastated by a feeling of emptiness. If she has any realization of what has happened, she will search for something to do—which is what she should have started preparing for long since. Some women have found new gratification in entering "secondary mothering roles" by fulfilling their own emotional needs in volunteer work in children's hospitals, orphanages, or nursery schools.

Idle mothers are far from the only result of the departure of children from home. It becomes a time of severe test for many a marriage, when husbands and wives go into a kind of shock on discovering that they do not really know each other. Dr. Charles Kramer, director of the Family Institute of Chicago, notes that such couples sometimes discover they are coming to each other as strangers at this point in their lives. "Instead of turning to each other and building a better, or in some case even a new, life together, they frequently seek unhealthy ways of doing things: alcoholism, extramarital affairs, neurotic behavior of various kinds."

Divorce is the answer in cases where the sudden loss of parental responsibility leaves a couple with little in common. "Twenty-year fracture" is the way sociologists describe this breakup. The problem is growing, according to statistics compiled by Dr. Alfred A. Messer, a psychiatrist at Emory University's Medical School in Atlanta. He blames this in part on our child-oriented society. "We are living in the century of the child, where the children become a nucleus around which most activities revolve," Dr. Messer writes, adding that child-oriented parents look to their offspring for emotional gratification, so that when the nest is vacated, the parents can neither satisfy each other nor adjust to each other.

As has been pointed out, every woman knows the day

her first child is born that eventually she will be out of a job. Therefore, if she has any wisdom at all, she will anticipate the day her last child leaves home and prepare for it by developing interests and building resources through volunteer work, a part-time job, women's clubs activities, and civic service. She might plan to return to college or attend business school and put to good use her gift of new time for the things she has always wanted to do but has not done, such as attending lectures and concerts and reading. In other words, this is her opportunity to catch up with her husband, make herself more interesting to him, and build a life of excitement, interest, and involvement that includes him.

As one woman said, "I've just discovered that I'm married to a very interesting man. We used to spend most of our time discussing Mary's school marks, Tim's music lessons, and the cost of feeding four people. Now we talk about my history class, his clients, the state of the world, and the political campaign. It's great fun."

ROLE REVERSAL—THE OTHER GENERATION GAP

Longevity can be a boon, but it also creates burdens, particularly when old people become financially dependent on their children or so disabled and senile that they cannot take care of themselves. This frequently is the family situation when a couple are well into their forties and fifties, financing college and planning for their retirement. The lack of understanding between aged parent and middle-aged child has created a growing generation gap that can be as troublesome as the breach between parents and teenagers—and often lasts much longer.

Dr. James Peterson, writing in *Married Love in the Middle Years*, summarized it neatly when he said: "We are called upon to be parents to our parents and have difficulty reversing our attitudes." This results from the fact that many parents have lost confidence in their own judgment as they have aged. They resent the time their children take from them, and, Dr. Peterson adds, "There is misunderstanding because our values have changed considerably from those that moved us during adolescence. We are impatient with the world in which our parents move."

All kinds of problems can result when an elderly parent goes to live with "the children." The grandparent may become so dependent on the entire family that he begins making constant demands, or his needs may be so great that he requires attention without asking for it. After years of being independent, a woman of middle years may now feel threatened by the presence of her mother. Or she might revert to her childhood relationship with her or suffer from a recurrence of damaging guilt feelings.

It can be even more difficult for children to grow up in the same household as their grandparents, under certain conditions. One of the authors was reared by her grandmother and had the advantage of the presence of her great-grandmother in the home for several years, which, while it presented some problems, was really a boon in the long run by providing a living link to the past. Many young people today do not seem to have any such ties with earlier generations; they do not hear firsthand accounts of what life was like when aged relatives were young or reap the fruits of their experience. They not only want everything now, but they think everything *is* now. Life-styles are different enough today so that conflicts of tempo, interests, and, yes, noise levels, need to be considered when a family is contemplating a haven for Grandma or Grandpa. On the other hand, most elderly people do not want to live with their married children and grandchildren if they can avoid it.

We cannot look upon the aged as inhumanely as was the practice in primitive societies, when they were left out to die. Our older people become ill and lonely. They need companionship and attention. Some of their needs are met by pension plans, Social Security, Medicare, welfare benefits, and private funds; nursing homes provide an answer for the infirm. But what is needed is not what dollars and cents can provide; it is the personal concern of a loved one, which has the greatest meaning in times of loneliness, depression, or need. The hunger for human contact has been poignantly demonstrated by the Help Line Telephone Center in New York, which provides around-the-clock counseling and advice on any subject you can name. During its first year of operation, nearly 100,000 men, women, and children called for help. A large number telephoned only because they were lonely and wanted to hear the sound of another voice. And most of these people were aged, alone in the big city, without a soul to turn to.

Until recent years, there was a stigma to having aged parents move into an "old folks' home." It is true that there are some shoddily run establishments, but most are operated by conscientious people. Today, with houses smaller than they were and fewer families aided by servants, a variety of accommodations for the elderly are available and desirable. They range from retirement communities where the "senior citizens" own their own cottages or rent apartments constructed with the infirmities of age in mind to hospital-like nursing homes for those who cannot look after themselves.

Another element enters the picture, and it cannot be overemphasized: finances. Unless a family is wealthy, the cost of nursing-home care is either prohibitive or eats up a couple's lifetime savings. However, the government has decreed that children do not have to be financially liable for their parents, and there are provisions in a number of states for the taxpayers to assume the burden. Those who cry "we can't take charity" may not be realistic in their reaction, for in a society where we are lengthening life without improving it very much in its later stages, we must assume a social responsibility for our elderly, most of whom have been taxpayers themselves during their lifetimes.

In any case, a couple trying to decide how their parents should spend the rest of their lives can find themselves in a profound conflict. Should we find room for Mom in our home, after all she has done for us? Should we finance an apartment in a senior citizens' development? Would a nursing home be the right place for her? It usually falls to the wife to make the decisions and arrangements, in the course of which she can become ridden with guilt, in part because of her own secret fears that the way in which she treats her parents will serve as an example for her children when she reaches her dotage.

BEING A MOTHER-IN-LAW IS NO JOKE

At the same time a woman becomes a parent to her parents, she may be going through still other role changes. A daughter or son gets married, and she finds she is a mother-in-law and, sooner or later, a grandmother as well. Stereotypes of these roles may both haunt and inhibit her unless she learns to avoid the pitfalls they can place in her path.

Even though today's mothers-in-law and grandmothers are younger, more independent, and more attractive and vigorous than ever, a woman cast in those roles is likely to cringe as she remembers the jokes that made *mother-in-law* a term of derision. A study made in the 1950s produced conclusions that most "in-law" troubles could be laid to the female of the species—that wives complained more than their husbands about their mothers-in-law, that mothers-in-law caused more trouble than fathers-in-law, and that sisters-in-law were more abrasive than brothers-in-law.

In a booklet, *How to Be a Good Mother-in-Law and Grandmother,* Edith G. Neisser points to some of the hazards. "Inescapable pulls and tensions are part and parcel of your feelings toward the people your children marry, and their feelings toward you," she maintains. She lists four reasons for resenting a mother-in-law:

1. She may be the ideal that a daughter-in-law feels she can never emulate.

2. Her son-in-law or daughter-in-law is angry with her because of a feeling she has never understood his or her mate.

3. She is blamed for her son's or daughter's shortcomings.

4. She is a scapegoat. The spouse of her child transfers to her his feelings of hatred toward his own parents.

To ease tensions, Mrs. Neisser recommends that the mother-in-law try to be flexible, recognize her children's rights to make their own decisions, regard them and their spouses as a unit and refuse to take sides in their quarrels, refrain from stirring up trouble, accept them as they are, go easy with suggestions, be discreet, and accept the fact that she is an in-law.

One way to avoid friction in the family is to limit the number and duration of visits a woman makes to her children. She should be especially careful about drop-in calls and would be well advised to telephone or write whenever she would like to see them. In most cases, it is best to wait for an invitation, and when a stay in the home is involved, an understanding should be reached at the outset as to its duration. There is an old saying that relatives, like fish, get pretty ripe after three or four days. Mothers-in-law might give this some thought before packing to visit their married children unless they are really smart and can afford to stay at a nearby hotel.

Being a grandmother presents some of the same problems as being a mother-in-law, except that they are compounded by a double age gap. More caution and restraint are needed to keep from meddling or flaunting wisdom and experience. Because of Grandma's years of carrying the responsibility for bringing up her children, it is sometimes difficult for her to remember that she does not have the final responsibility for the grandchildren, and sometimes she needs to caution Grandpa against meddling. On the other side of this well-worn coin is the need for Grandma to set some limits of her own; she is not going to be a baby-sitter. On occasion, she would be delighted to have the grandchildren as guests, but not on a regular basis. The young parents can hire someone for that chore.

When youngsters go to visit Grandma, they have open to them a relationship they cannot have at home. The grandmother may have more time to devote to the youngsters. She is less harassed and pressured and takes time to listen to what they have to say and enjoy their company in a relaxed way. In doing this she has to put up a guard against getting too involved in their lives or coming between them and their parents.

Whatever she does, she need not yield to the temptation to demand that she be appreciated for her efforts. Marriage counselors tend to advise mothers-in-law as well as grandmothers not to expect expressions of gratitude for gifts. Young couples and their children want to accept what is given, provided there are no strings attached, but they really want to stand on their own and are likely to resent having to accept anything from relatives. Resentment and ingratitude are not very pleasant reactions to generosity, but they are classical responses, whether the parties involved are two nations or two people. For the sake of long-range harmony, a certain amount of ungraciousness must be overlooked.

"There are certain difficulties involved in being a mother-in-law or grandmother that can probably never be completely overcome," Mrs. Neisser warns, "but with an awareness of those hazards, it is possible through what you say and do to reduce and prevent some tensions."

It should go without saying that relationships with one's children and grandchildren are bound to be smoother and richer if they are not the sole source of human relationship and gratification for an older woman. Today's woman should be able to fill her life with enough friends, cultural interests, and community activities to keep her from being emotionally dependent on her children and grandchildren—and a burden to herself.

CHAPTER
6

Women Alone: The Widowed, Divorced, and Unmarried

SHE SHUDDERED as she turned the key in the lock. The house was dark, no cheery "Hi, there!" to greet her. For the first time in twenty-five years, she was really alone. After the funeral she had gone home with her married daughter for a few weeks, but now she was facing up to the fact that she was—the word was the most difficult she had ever had to say—she was a widow! Despite family and friends and the warm memories, she was a woman alone.

While her husband had not left her wealthy, he had managed to build financial security and, unlike many men, he had kept her fully informed of his financial obligations and arrangements. She knew where the safe-deposit box and the key to it were and where he kept his bankbooks and his will. His lawyer was an old friend, and between them they had rounded up all the details on his insurance, his investments, where and how the mortgage payments were to be made, and other necessary information.

She realized she did not have to worry about finances,

but she was concerned about other aspects of her future. What should she do with herself? Friends and family were plying her with all kinds of advice. "Sell the house and move back into the city." "Don't sell the house and break old ties." "Get a job." "Don't get a job—find volunteer work instead." "Take a long trip." "Travel right now would be bad for you."

After listening patiently and silently to well-meaning suggestions, she did what many other women have wisely decided to do. Nothing. She made up her mind to wait a year before making any important moves. While she might find a job or look for a useful and interesting volunteer activity, she was not going to pull up stakes for the time being. She would try to pick up the pieces of her life right where she was, get to know herself better, and avoid jumping into anything in haste.

Soon friends started inviting her to lunch, dinner, the club, and bridge parties and offered activities to keep her occupied. She accepted every one she could, not always because she really wanted to go out but because she dreaded the thought of developing the habit of sitting at home alone, where she might start feeling sorry for herself. Sometimes her friends invited a widower, a bachelor, or a divorced man to make the table come out even. That was pleasant, but she did not want to think about another marriage right now. Often when the men drove her home, they made elaborate passes, obviously thinking she was starved for love and affection—*their* love and affection—and would be easy prey. She managed to fend off the advances, but it was difficult, and not one of the men ever asked her out after that. "Oh, well," she mused, "that's *their* problem, not mine."

In time the telephone rang less often and the invitations dwindled, even though she entertained frequently to pay back her social obligations. She came to realize—without a trace of self-pity—that widows can be a drag.

People weary of being concerned about them and looking after their social welfare. Then too she had detected twinges of jealousy on the part of some of her friends when their husbands paid special attention to her. A few hackles were raised when she asked a neighbor to fix her power mower, and the local gossips lost no time in spreading the word—falsely—that she was after the men in the neighborhood, and wasn't it a pity because her husband had been such a nice family man.

These were not serious problems, but they nettled. And so, at the end of a year, she decided to go back to college for refresher courses and perhaps a master's degree and return to the teaching career she had left for marriage. She sold the house, invested the proceeds, and moved into an apartment in a college town, where she made new friends in the academic community and launched a social life of her own making, with plenty of dates with men far more interesting than those she had known in suburbia.

That story represents a composite of the experiences of many women who have found themselves widowed in young middle age, still attractive and active, and able and willing to build new lives. Similar experiences have been encountered by divorcées, but their road to adjustment is often more difficult because they are more likely to have unpleasant memories of the marital breakup and to have stored away bitterness that needs to be dispelled before they can function smoothly again. If the divorce has been the husband's idea, there may be the element of rejection, which is demoralizing to a woman and sometimes leaves permanent scars. If she has brought suit, her feelings about men may be harsh, at least for the time being. Although at middle age a woman is unlikely to have any young children, she may have teenagers to look after or youngsters in college, and her financial position may be tenuous if she is dependent on alimony payments. Her chances for a stable social life with her old friends are even less than those of her widowed neighbor because divorcées pose greater threats in the minds of married women and are more likely to be censured than pitied.

Beyond that, women alone who have had men in their lives have a number of adjustments to make, particularly those who find themselves footloose again in middle age.

For the mature woman who has never been married there are some of the same problems, and a whole set of different ones as well. She may feel insecure because of finances; unless she has been left a legacy or has been able to plan her security, she is likely to suffer from attacks of depression or desperation or feel rejected. She is more truly alone than many of the divorced and widowed, but at the same time, she does not have the same problem of adjusting to this aloneness. Many single women live with other spinsters or take care of older parents, and while the end of such relationships can produce desolation, the need to adjust to the sudden departure of a man from the household is not there.

THE OVERALL PICTURE

Women alone—widows, divorcées, and the unmarried—constitute a significant segment of the American population. One of every eight women—more than ten million—are widows, outnumbering widowers by more than four to one, according to the Bureau of the Census. Most are past middle age, with one out of twenty aged fifty-five to sixty-four, two out of every five sixty-five to seventy-four, and seven out of ten past seventy-five. Two of three widows have their own households; as the financial wizards like to point out, women hold the purse strings on most of the nation's wealth.

The number of divorced women is larger. Forty-one

per cent of American marriages end in divorce. Although many of the people involved marry again, a significant number remain alone for the rest of their lives.

The number of "bachelor girls" is estimated at fifteen million, most of them under thirty-five. However, a large proportion of the nearly one million who are above that age are unlikely to marry and can be classified as women alone.

The woman who has remained single frequently encounters more problems with aging than does the well-adjusted married woman. She may be beset with fears about the time when she will not be able to work or becomes ill or infirm with little savings and no family. There are compensations—fewer responsibilities and household cares and more satisfaction in the world of work—but the spinster tends to feel cheated. She does not belong to anyone, which makes it difficult for her to find the emotional stability she needs.

Although the single woman generally leads an active life and has a variety of interests, these may not have helped her hurdle the obstacles of maturity. It has been said that the unhappiest woman of all is the unmarried executive or supervisor between forty-five and fifty-five who lives an organization life, acting on the subconscious message that it is now or never for her.

WHAT AN EXPERT SAYS

Advice to the woman alone abounds. Some of it is offered by authorities on the subject—professionals or women who have "been there" themselves. One of those who has counseled many women is Dr. Mary Jane Hungerford, of the American Institute for Family Relations in Los Angeles, who finds that women alone after forty, whether divorced, widowed, or spinsters, have problems no matter how uncomplicated their lives might be, or have been.

Two words are at the core of her message to the aging single female: *Keep living.* If a woman has a variety of interests, life will go well because activities lead to friends and friends lead to new romances—or at least to an interesting social life. As far as Dr. Hungerford is concerned, the worst thing a woman can do is sit back and *wait* for something to happen, because it seldom does without some initiative, even if it only entails picking up the telephone to invite friends to dinner.

Some of the most miserable widows we have known are the richest, while some of the happiest get along on very little. One example that comes to mind is that of a widowed teacher living on a small income who is able to say: "I think of myself as a survivor on a desert island. I don't have everything I want or need, but by invention I can manage to supply my wants, and I am determined to enjoy everything more for that reason. If tomorrow never comes, I've had today, and I haven't wasted an instant of it."

There you see a lucky woman—luckier than many, especially many of those Dr. Hungerford counsels. She begins the process by recommending vocational tests for the woman who has been cast adrift, either never having worked or having been out of the labor market so long that her skills are rusty. After finding a desirable direction in which to move, a return to school may be indicated before it is advisable to apply for work. The many who have held jobs before marriage or have been widowed or divorced before are more likely to be able to look after themselves than were their mothers and grandmothers when they found themselves without a breadwinner. Another factor in the growing self-reliance of women lies in the fact that husbands are not around home as much as they used to be; a goodly proportion put in long days commuting or are required to travel extensively, leaving wives more on their own.

A woman suddenly alone should know how to deal with a bank as well as a leaky faucet. She should have some idea of what is entailed in consulting a stockbroker, seeing that the car is properly maintained, and keeping up the house. She certainly is capable of going to a restaurant, doing the shopping, and calling the plumber or electrician. However, she is likely to need some financial guidance because, as we have indicated, husbands do not always keep their wives as fully aware of family finances as they should.

It is Dr. Hungerford's belief that most women over forty stand good chances of finding love and companionship *if they want it.* The men available among the divorced and widowed are going to be attracted by the most outgoing women. If a woman is interesting, people will be interested in her; Dr. Hungerford says it is mainly a matter of her attending to business, keeping active, and staying in the mainstream of life—something many women are reluctant to do, particularly if they have no financial worries.

It may come as a surprise to a woman suddenly thrust into the role of a "single" that, at the age of forty and beyond, the dating pattern is quite unlike that of her teens or college years. The mature woman can be more aggressive and she need not be so hesitant in trying to meet men casually under conditions that would be frowned upon if her daughter or granddaughter tried them. Nor need she have any hangups about having a sex life without marriage, although if interests and activities jibe, companionship without sex frequently occurs.

In addition to being brought together by friends, the mature couple often meet at church or through volunteer work for a social agency or hospital. They may be engaged in community activity, such as the city council or politics, or find one another on the golf links. Some women Dr.

Hungerford knows have sought public activities and service out of a desire to draw upon their own experiences and ideas in the hope of influencing society. They take up golf or tennis for the physical well-being that will accrue, with the social aspects a fringe benefit. A strictly social life may be the least likely area for finding eligible men. Convinced that it is a waste of time to try to meet men who live in the same community solely through social encounters, Dr. Hungerford advises a sorting out of interests, meeting a man wherever men may be—watching the ticker in a brokerage office, attending night school, playing tennis or golf, taking dancing lessons, or joining a walking club, for example. A season ticket to the symphony may strike a responsive chord. Going on the prowl for a man in clubs, bars, or public dance halls can be degrading, however. True, many women have done it with success, but the chances are slim of meeting someone with common interests.

Dr. Hungerford is not a prude who frowns on pickups, which she acknowledges often blossom into romance, but she warns that a woman may be exploited by the man she meets casually in a laundromat or museum or some other public place. The ending is often sad because the ingredient of congeniality may be lacking. While the middle-aged widow will be more resistant to and fussier about the men she meets—and particularly *where* she meets them—if she had a good marriage, the divorcée may now be eager to take a few risks.

The idea of computer dating causes Dr. Hungerford to raise her eyebrows in skepticism unless a woman is desperate. She maintains that the system does not work in most cases because it seems to be impossible to program a machine to pinpoint areas of congeniality. Their batting average is high when it comes to matching such hard facts as education and economic and cultural status, but the computerized date seekers' personalities are too elusive to cause any lights to flash or bells to ring.

At the same time any single woman should bear in mind that every eligible man who asks for a date is not necessarily a potential husband. As Dr. Hungerford says, "There is nothing that gets in your way more than going out to *find* someone to marry." Rather, the idea is be an interesting person, make the most of every day, and enjoy the people who pop up along the way. Whether they are eligible or not, it is possible to have a good time with them.

With all her social and business activities, a woman alone does have periods of loneliness. Dr. Paul Tournier, a Swiss psychiatrist, has called it "the most devastating malady of the age." Psychiatric patients acknowledge that loneliness is the main reason they seek help; many have become alcoholics or have contemplated suicide because of the nagging ache. Perhaps the saddest cases are those of the aged who feel useless and unwanted. For the lonely, Dr. Billy Graham, the evangelist, offers a three-step cure: recognize loneliness as an enemy, a disease that erodes happiness and "sours and sickens the spirit"; learn to tell the difference between being alone and being lonely, accepting the fact that many productive, creative people have to do their work alone; and ease your boredom by becoming involved in service to others. Another famous clergyman, Dr. Norman Vincent Peale, urges the lonely to devote part of each day to thinking about other people and doing things for them.

A WIDOW SPEAKS FROM EXPERIENCE

Out of the experiences of women who have been widowed, guidelines can be drawn for coping with this crisis. Isabella Taves, author of a book entitled *Women Alone* and the widow of Dan Mich, editor of *Look* magazine, told us that when her husband died, she was strongly tempted to leave New York, where she had lived for twenty years, and "go home" to Lincoln, Nebraska; but a wise aunt, speaking out of her own experience, insisted, "Make no major decisions the first year." Miss Taves accepted the advice and has never regretted it.

"That first year is not an easy year," she recalled, "but it's a very worthwhile year. You grow enormously. If you are bright, it's a good year for you. It's a year in which you talk honestly and deeply to people you know and trust, people who love you. If you are not a strong woman, you don't try; if you don't really make a struggle, it's a year in which you can founder. You have to go through a bad period in order to emerge and you do everything possible to make that year better. But you don't turn against it. You look it in the face."

Miss Taves advises the woman who stays put for a year to take several short vacations to "blur memories." As part of her process of learning to be on her own, she should make her own reservations and plan her own itinerary, but she may be in for trouble if she sets out on the "dream vacation" she and her husband had always planned; it would be a constant and painful reminder of him. As far as Miss Taves is concerned, it is also a mistake to travel with a woman friend. She prefers going it alone, doing what she wants, and meeting people along the way.

Speaking further from her own experience, Miss Taves observed that widows and divorcées share feelings of rejection. Fearful of a social stigma, they suffer from pangs of guilt because they have been taught that a woman is supposed to hold a marriage together. "I had dreams right after my husband died that we were back in the courting stage," she recounted, "and he would not marry me. If that isn't rejection, what is it?"

Finances are the overriding factor in being able to stick to a determination to stand pat for the first year of widowhood. Some women find they cannot afford to continue to live in the same place, but for that crucial year, even a move should be considered as an interim step, not a final commitment. Miss Taves favors the city for the woman alone because it offers more things to do—the theater, concerts, museums, and clubs, to name a few. In suburbia it is difficult to find outlets and friends of different ages. An exception, of course, is the woman who is dedicated to her home and is willing to settle for a restricted social life with old friends; she probably will be happier staying put. However, she may have to accept the fact that there are too many single women in the world—and almost no available men in suburbia—and that her friends really do not want her around as much as they did when she had a mate. Once she realizes this, she can build a life for herself by being helpful to older, more lonesome people and making herself available to give reassurance and advice to younger ones.

There are pitfalls to avoid, the principal one in Miss Taves's opinion being the "mamaism" syndrome—the mother who leans too heavily on her son. Daughters do not encounter this problem as often as their brothers, says Miss Taves, who cited the case of a widow who destroyed her son's marriage by staying near him and making a pest of herself by summoning him to do repair jobs or take her to the movies and otherwise monopolizing his free time (perhaps she really wanted him back under her thumb).

Another woman Miss Taves mentioned had been the "baby doll" type when she was married to a brilliant lawyer who did not think she could do anything useful other than cook and push a vacuum cleaner. She became an excellent cook and housekeeper and was a dutiful mother. When her husband died unexpectedly, he did not leave her with much income, having been convinced—as are a lot of other people—that he was going to live forever. His baby doll had to get a job. She started as a saleswoman in a store and eventually moved into the publicity department. In the course of her business progress, she became a new woman and married a man far more attractive and understanding than her first husband and one who made her feel more like a person.

Helpless housewives seem to abound. Miss Taves recalled another she knew in Lincoln. The woman accepted the role of dependency against her better judgment, always deferring to her husband, never asking about finances or any other family matters. One day she discovered that he was a tax dodger. She divorced him, managed to pay his taxes for him, and supported their three children; he disappeared, as do about 100,000 other men every year who simply pick up and move out without a word.

The woman went back to the advertising copywriting job she held before marriage and eventually was placed in charge of the company's West Coast office. She is enjoying life, but she remains suspicious of men.

Her experience bolsters Miss Taves's view that life as a woman alone can be full and happy *if one keeps busy.* She is convinced that it can be a mistake to remarry too soon, before having a chance to discover oneself, and she is wary of the further pitfall of settling for anyone just to get married. She gave a few helpful hints on how to get the inside track in the race for the hand of an eligible widower who suddenly finds himself without someone to take care of his laundry and cook his meals. Because he does not know what to do with himself, he is likely to marry again within three months—and perhaps live to regret it. Miss Taves's advice is, therefore: If you know a recent widower or divorced man and you *want* to marry him, catch him within three months—before he finds out where he should take his suits to be cleaned. The man who manages to survive bachelorhood during this critical period may smarten up about designing women; after he learns to cook and can find his way to the nearest Chinese laundry, he may decide he does not need to marry again (he will be in the minority, however).

Miss Taves, like other widows, has encountered some difficulty with married men, and she remains surprised at the number of otherwise respectable husbands who make passes at single women. The logical conclusion she has reached is that they apparently succeed in many cases, particularly during the first vulnerable year when a widow does not know how to fend off passes and needs a man around so much that she may say yes when she really means no.

Discussing widowhood in *Women Alone,* Miss Taves observed that self-respect can become more important than happiness to the single woman. In interviews with women across the country, she found that happiness, rather than being a goal, is a by-product and often a fleeting one. "It can vanish during a pleasant evening with friends, and send you scuttling home to draw your blinds and shut out the sight of other families together. Yet a chance conversation on the street, an encounter at the bank, a telephone call or a letter from an old friend will send spirits soaring."

Miss Taves told us about something that has helped her and might help others. "When I was married," she said, "there were several things that my husband didn't care about my doing." He did not like her to wear much makeup or low-cut dresses and he frowned on very short skirts. "I have maybe gone too far," she admitted, "but I have worn low-cut dresses for the first time in my life and I have been wearing my skirts very short. This is good for my morale even if I come back to my senses later."

HINTS FROM A WIDOW'S WIDOW

Mrs. Marian Champagne has seen widowhood from both sides—as a widow and as a lawyer with widows for clients. In her book *Facing Life Alone,* she begins with the first fact a widow must deal with after the funeral:

money, or the lack of it. How much money she has determines her life-style. Then come other elements such as her age, her health, her education, and her ambition. How many dependents does she have, and how old are her children? Regardless of her situation, Mrs. Champagne, like others, advises that she delay vital decisions whenever possible.

"My advice is, whatever you are thinking of doing right away, don't," she told us. "Cool it. Just cool it. Most of the decisions made by widows in the first few weeks are made in panic."

Although divorcées and widows share many problems, there are some important differences. Mrs. Champagne finds that the divorcée usually is on the defensive against a society that tells her: "You had a husband and you let him go; it's your own fault." The widow hears a lot of "Oh, you poor thing." Both, Mrs. Champagne believes, have to learn to think of themselves as persons, "not one blade of a pair of scissors that no longer will cut anything." Not only must they cope with finances and often serve as father as well as mother, but they also must build a social life in which they try not to cling to old friends as a "fifth wheel" or go to the other extreme of sitting at home knitting and watching television because "nobody wants me anymore."

"The widow must avoid the worst possible trap," Mrs. Champagne warns, "which is self-pity, the feeling that the world owes her something because she has suffered."

Any single woman who is reasonably attractive is bound to be regarded as a menace by some of her married friends. When a widow laments that "nobody invites me anymore," Mrs. Champagne has a difficult time explaining to her that women who have shaky marriages are afraid to have a husbandless woman around lest a flirtation develop. Then too, the fact that a woman has become able to live alone successfully rattles some married couples, particularly the wives, when they see that it is possible to make it without a man. Some husbands, who regard the single woman as a bad influence on their wives, especially if she dresses in the latest fashions and buys a new car every year or two, may fear that their wives will feel trapped when they see how free and happy another woman can *appear* to be without being committed to one man.

"The loner simply has got to make a world of her own," Mrs. Champagne said, "and not continue leaning on her former friends, and for this reason it is often a good idea for her to sell her house in the suburbs and move back to the city. The suburbs are cruelly hard on a woman alone because they exist for families—complete families. If there is no husband coming home at six o'clock every night, life is simply too bleak."

Mrs. Champagne recalled a client whose husband left an estate of $500,000—a tidy sum, to be sure—but because she had never been allowed to handle money, she had no idea what it meant. Fearing she would not be able to pay the taxes, she thought she would have to sell her modest suburban three-bedroom ranch house and move to smaller quarters. Better heads prevailed, however, and she was persuaded not to do anything until she could come to the realization that she was in a sound financial position and could stay where she was until she decided what she really wanted to do.

That woman learned, as others do, that relatives are not always the best sources of advice. It is difficult for them to be objective, particularly if they have a financial stake. A lawyer is the best possible source of a wide range of advice, including words of wisdom about dealing with the relatives. One trap in the path of the newly widowed is set by members of the family who think that now that Poor Jane is alone she might find solace in taking care of doddery old Aunt Minnie or a young orphaned cousin.

Relatives also lurk in the wings when the family heirlooms are being sold, offering to buy prized pieces for almost nothing while really expecting them as gifts.

For the woman whose husband had a lawyer, the search for legal advice is at an end. But if there has been no family lawyer, a widow would be wise to find a stranger rather than her husband's club crony, a neighbor, or a relative, all of whom are too involved with her problems. Unfortunately, there are some lawyers who prey on widows with a little money. The local bar association or Legal Aid Society usually has a list of reputable attorneys. Or you might consult your clergyman or physician for a recommendation.

In evaluating her financial situation, a woman has to consider not only her basic way of life but also some of the fringe expenditures. Does she want and need a car? What should she do about the clubs she has belonged to for years? Can she afford them, and will she continue to benefit from membership? How should she react when the annual charity appeals fill her mailbox? Should she stop contributing or give less? Mrs. Champagne has noted that many widows contribute more than they can afford because they are ashamed to say their budgets will no longer permit philanthropies. But if a widow has a lawyer, she can say: "I would love to give, but my lawyer doesn't let me do anything without asking him."

When it comes to considering a job, full or part time, a woman with no previous experience in the workaday world should move with caution. She might consider, "What am I better at than most of my friends?" Or she might ask the opinions of friends and relatives about her special talents. One way to clarify possibilities is to make a list of one's talents. Almost any woman who has reared a family could qualify for practical nursing. With a minimum of training, a woman would make a proficient hairdresser or stenographer. A sales job or a position as a receptionist would not require any special skills.

While it is difficult for a woman to plan ahead for widowhood, Mrs. Champagne is convinced that every girl should be required to work before she gets married. In an emergency she can brush up on her skills and plunge back into the labor market with a minimum of reentry problems. Volunteer work can lead to a job when it is needed. If a woman who has been a loyal worker goes to an official of her pet charity and tells him she now needs work, he certainly will consider her for the next staff opening. Job guidance can also be sought from men who knew her husband—Rotarians, Lions, Kiwanians, or whatever. They will want to help George's widow if they can. Clergymen also hear about openings, and many companies, particularly in the direct-selling business, actually conduct searches for "mature" women who want to build new careers.

LIFE WITHOUT FATHER

When Howard Lindsay, the noted coauthor and star of *Life with Father,* one of Broadway's most successful plays, died, his widow, the actress Dorothy Stickney, decided to try to go on living in much the same style she had when he was alive. She found no great conflict between running a house and having a career. "There are a lot of things you suddenly are faced with—responsibilities that you haven't really been aware of before, suddenly there are all sorts of large and small decisions that you have to make, and then occasionally, it does get to be a problem," she told us.

"I love our house. Howard and I lived here for twenty-two years, and when Howard first died, people would say to me occasionally, 'Well, what are you going to do now, Dorothy? Where are you going to live?'

"I know the impulse is to run away. I think it's the biggest mistake in the world. I don't think women should rush to make any great big changes when they suddenly find themselves alone. Wait a little while. I have gotten over the dread of opening the front door, and I love being here now. It gives me a feeling of shelter."

Miss Stickney found that her greatest comfort in her grief lay in friends who had also lost their husbands. They rallied around with assurances of the one thing that is difficult to believe—"that it *will* get better and that you *will* survive, and that the time *will* come when your life will have some meaning again. It is true. You wouldn't believe it if you hadn't heard it from some of your friends who have survived the thing. I mean women who had long and good marriages. That was a great thing for me.

"Then there are lots of other helps. At first you put one day after another and have a great deal that has to be done. That is a great thing. First you're sort of in shock; then you gradually begin to learn about things, and the responsibilities that you did not have when your husband was alive take up a lot of your time—and should.

"There are lots of things I'm interested in. I love my house. I have the dearest, kindest friends in the world. I think it is terribly important for women whose husbands have died to *let* their friends be good to them. Go out, go with your friends to dinner whether you feel like it or not. Don't just crawl into your shell and say, 'I don't feel like going out tonight.' It's better to go even if you don't want to. I'm sure of that!"

Having a career can be a great comfort, and Miss Stickney regards herself as fortunate in being able to continue her work in the theater. "One does survive any kind of grief or loss," she says. "One does. One thinks one won't, but one does, and things *do* get better, they *do* get easier, and it is fortunate if you have responsibilities. If you don't, I think you ought to go out and get some."

THE NOT-SO-GAY DIVORCÉE

Much of what has been said about widows applies also to divorcées, with important differences. The divorced or separated woman often hides from married friends and relatives or is reluctant to discuss her feelings. She becomes part of what sociologists call a "subculture of the formerly married," with its distinct feelings, moral values, and behavior patterns; its members live in their own world within the bigger world, have their own social life, and are less likely to be inhibited about having sexual relations than they were before marriage. The formerly married tend to gravitate toward one another, even at crowded cocktail parties. With their own special kind of radar, they may "look available" by their manner of appraising others to see if they are "in the market." The messages fly—and sometimes produce results.

The divorced woman seldom gets any real help from friends and relatives, who introduce her to men they feel are "safe," with the result that the men are often too dull, too conservative, too respectable, or too old. Such encounters send divorcées in search of other sources of manpower—organizations of the formerly married, resort hotels, cruises, groups that attract unattached members of both sexes, country clubs, tours for singles, etc.

Women over forty have a more difficult time getting dates than do their male contemporaries, who always seem to be in demand. It is easier for a middle-aged man to find companionship with someone younger. The forty-ish woman may be handicapped further by her reluctance to risk being hurt again or by setting impossible standards, which are her subconscious expression of fear of another failure. She fears rejection as well as failure, but she still needs to get into circulation, which means taking some chances, going places where she can meet people, mainly men, striking up acquaintances, accepting invitations for dates, fully aware that something untoward might happen, but hoping for the best. In other words, she needs to develop self-assurance, learn to like herself better, and be willing to gamble on new relationships.

As we have pointed out, the divorcée is not usually as welcome as the widow on the doorsteps of old friends, who tend to shy away from one whose marriage has failed. This reaction sprouts mainly from a sense of insecurity among wives. When the divorcée remarries, however, she is welcomed back into the fold, since she is no longer a potential threat.

It is difficult to accept, but the divorcée must understand that some women really do fear that their husbands may want to play around. If she accepts it, she can take countermeasures by inviting her married friends to dinner, always making sure to have a single man to serve as her cohost. It helps too when a divorcée can appear at parties with an escort she has found for herself. This neutralizes her position; the threat is minimized.

WHY OLD MARRIAGES DIE

Problems surrounding divorced women are growing because the "twenty-year fracture," middle-age breakup, is becoming more common. More than 25 per cent of all failures occur after more than fifteen years of marriage, and the rate is accelerating, according to Dr. Alfred A. Messer, professor of psychiatry at Emory University Medical School in Atlanta. He gives several reasons, including an increasing acceptance of divorce and liberalization of divorce laws; greater affluence, which is making women more independent financially; and a general deterioration of the institution of marriage.

As we have pointed out, in the old days families lived close enough together so that one could always find a shoulder to cry on in times of crisis. Now they are so spread out that such solace is no longer available, and couples do not work as hard at resolving their differences.

Dr. Messer's first reason for an increase in middle-age breakups—greater acceptance of divorce—appears to be the most significant factor in the termination of long-term marriages, which usually have been deteriorating for years. Many couples who have survived years of married misery separate without getting divorces. No one knows just how many—or how many occupy the same house, or even the same bedroom, while going their separate ways. Dr. Messer notes that when age forty-five hits a couple in the face, one or both parties often decide that this is their last chance to strike a blow for freedom. Sometimes drinking is the cause of divorce, and the husband is not always the culprit; women alcoholics are far more numerous than is commonly thought because it is easy for them to be secret drinkers at home, and also because their families tend to shield them. Sometimes older parents move in and ultimately break up a marriage, or a child with problems becomes a bone of contention. Glandular changes also occur, causing personality deviations that engender desires to revolt, to "live just once before I die."

A woman's discontent with life in general may focus on her husband, and she can become enraged by baffling changes in him. Sometimes a man's career alters radically in middle age—for better or for worse—or levels off. This too can affect a marriage. Vocational problems may create financial pressure and fears of failure that cast a pall. Success can trigger crises, particularly for a marriage that can somehow weather adversity but not prosperity. In those instances more leisure time and more money contribute to less togetherness and more adult delinquency; they make extramarital affairs economically feasible.

Dr. Messer said in an interview that society has long held the erroneous notion that the longer a couple are married, the longer they will remain so. That has not been true of many couples who have gone to him for help. In fact, the rate at which marriages of fifteen or more years break up has doubled in the last two decades, he noted, with the most critical time coming shortly after the last child has left home. The parents have found their satisfactions, their interests, their fulfillments, and their frustrations in their children; when the children depart, they leave a void behind.

Sociologists report that as many as a third of all brides are pregnant. This can nurture a lingering doubt on the part of the woman as to whether her husband would have married her otherwise. Frictions result; couples often stay together out of feelings of obligation to the child, or out of guilt, separating as soon as it is grown.

Dr. Messer advises couples who have been married twenty years to take a honeymoon trip. He urges them to become aware of the changes that have taken place in each other. A husband may have new interests that suddenly supplant his old love, football. Now he may prefer bridge or reading mystery novels. His wife should accommodate herself to the change, and he, in turn, needs to be aware of her evolving interests—painting, the piano, or bird-watching, instead of pursuits that were oriented to the children when they were growing up.

Divorce, at any age, can be and often is a good solution when differences are insurmountable. Dr. Albert Ellis, the noted psychotherapist, is one of those who advocate divorce at any time if the partners really are miserable. His first reaction is that they "finally got the guts to get a divorce." And he goes on to explain that "they've usually had problems long before, sometimes almost since the day of marriage. But they felt they had to stay with the marriage, sometimes because of the children, sometimes because of other affairs, sometimes for economic reasons. Now that they're over forty and the children are sufficiently grown up, the monetary matters may be better. By this age, they've decided they don't care that much what people—such as their parents—think. They're going to get a divorce, regardless!"

Such a marital collapse can be brought on more by changing attitudes toward individual freedom than by an actual worsening of the marriage, according to Dr. Ellis. Some people find that they have better sex lives outside marriage or that sex has been the only good thing about their relationships and they want something in addition.

Because those who consult Dr. Ellis at his Institute for Advanced Study in Rational Psychotherapy frequently tend to exaggerate their problems, he encourages them to analyze why they are upset about their marriages and then persuades them to discuss their feelings in enough depth to determine if divorce is an answer. In many cases Dr. Ellis manages to keep a couple together, "not because I am interested in marriage in itself," he explains, "but mainly because I am interested in human beings and getting them to be less upset, no matter what is happening. When they are less upset they frequently will be able to happily go on with the marriage." But, he adds, after they have calmed down, they may decide instead that divorce really is the answer.

TO BE OR NOT TO BE A BRIDE AGAIN

Remarriage is in the picture for a woman widowed or divorced in middle age if she *really* wants another husband. Whether they realize it or not, those who at least subconsciously do not want to marry again express their preference by avoiding situations in which they can meet eligible men. Marian Champagne noted instances in which women still *feel* married although they are widowed or divorced. Religious beliefs influence others who do not seek remarriage. There are widows who begin to enjoy their freedom—sexually and otherwise—and would rather not settle down again. Sometimes children or other relatives raise such storms of protest that the subject is dropped. Alimony plays a role for the divorcée who wants a man who can support her when the monthly payments stop at least as well as her ex-husband has. And there are widows and divorcées who were so miserable in their marriages that they do not want to try again. If the first husband was sick, a woman may equate being a wife with being a nurse; if he was drunk or abusive, she may fear a second husband will be at least as bad.

After the first shock of widowhood, a woman may find that she really enjoys doing what *she* pleases. If she does marry again, she stands a greater chance for happiness if she has learned first how to live alone. Most undesirable second marriages observed by Mrs. Champagne and others are rooted in desperation. A woman says: "I've got to grab a man. I'm left out of everything. Nobody invites me over. I'm a nothing. I've got to show the world that I can get a man." The worst possible marriages result, while good matches come from a feeling that "I am a person. I can live alone if I have to. I can live reasonably happily." The woman who feels that way finds a man she would like to live with because she hopes both of them will be happier.

"There is a feeling," Mrs. Champagne observed, "that as soon as you hear a man has been widowed, you must run after him, bring the casserole, go over and knock on the door, and insert yourself into his life, because widowers are notoriously dependent and can't go it alone, and you can grab one while he's still grieving. This is a very bad setup.

"Contrary to what people think, a man who marries on

the rebound is much too likely to be looking for his first wife all over again. This is not the way to start a second marriage."

He may keep his first wife's picture on the dresser, get her name confused with that of his new bride, or persist in comparing them. As an added thorn, his children may resent their stepmother, just as hers, even if they are grown, may chafe at having a new father.

Finances are another sensitive area in remarriage. Both parties should consider the matter as objectively and frankly as they can, with the help of their lawyers. The children of both need protection, although the prospective partners may want to make some provision for one another if their resources permit. If the bride-to-be is planning to invest in her husband's business, legal safeguards are needed to protect her estate. In addition, both parties should be able to prove that they are free to marry; many a bride—and bridegroom—have discovered belatedly that they are not legally wed. Once all of the details are attended to, a middle-age marriage can be more successful than a young one, possibly happier than either party anticipated, free of fears of pregnancy, of arguments over how many children they should have, of the obstacles of parents who object to their union. "And then," Mrs. Champagne added, "just living has taught you so much. You learn to share something besides a bed."

At any rate, there should be nothing to fear from a second marriage, which in most cases seems to work out quite well, according to Dr. Ben Schlesinger, professor at the School of Social Work at the University of Toronto, who has seen couples learn from a first marriage, even if it has failed. A good second marriage is more likely, of course, after a successful first match that has ended in widowhood. While there are women who feel that the life they had with their first husbands can never be repeated, most widows appear to make good adjustments to the second marriage, or so the experts say.

Recent studies indicate that a number of people marry for the second time in their sixties. While there may not be any prospects for matrimony in one's immediate social circle, men are available elsewhere, although it probably is inadvisable to move to another community solely to find a mate. Those Schlesinger has talked to have found spouses in clubs, through dating bureaus, and even in bars, or have been introduced by friends and relatives. "When they were ready," he observed, "they were able to meet somebody."

Interestingly, divorced men who remarry tend to choose spinsters somewhat younger than they, while the widower seeks out a widow closer to his own age. The divorcée is likely to marry a man who has been divorced. Schlesinger theorized that a widow is more comfortable with a man who has undergone a similar experience. A few perennial bachelors seek out widows with ready-made families—it makes them feel safer. While widows wait five or six years before remarrying, the divorcée stays single an average of two years. The widow may have her grief to work through, or, if she has had a good marriage, she may not be in a hurry to try again, whereas the divorcée often needs to prove to herself that she can be a success as a wife.

"The divorced person still is seen as a kind of—let's use the term *sexual prey*—in the sense that she has a kind of gay divorcée image, and it is true that friends and non-friends see her as a good partner to take to bed and approach her very frequently in this kind of way," Schlesinger said.

"The separated woman is neither fish nor fowl. She is a fifth wheel because she is neither married nor untangled. . . . She doesn't know what to do. Should she date or not? Is the separation final or not? If she does date or go out, will it be used against her in a future divorce action? She is in a dilemma.

"The widow, on the other hand, we approach with 'Oh, isn't it too bad that she's a widow!' Of course, if she's pretty and outgoing, I'm sure that men would make propositions but that might be a compliment."

While few young people apparently evaluate their reasons for getting married, couples contemplating mature matches often discuss the positive and negative aspects and take time to recognize each other's feelings. Important also, according to Schlesinger, is the fact that about 80 per cent of those who marry for the second time have shared the same bed beforehand, entering their unions better prepared sexually than they were the first time. He says that couples who have had long first marriages feel that they learned from their experiences and are able to enter their second marriages with more mature outlooks; they understand themselves and one another better.

Sometimes, however, it is difficult to forget the first marriage. It may even be impossible, but Schlesinger finds this a normal reaction that will be minimized if it is discussed frankly with a new spouse. "Do not be afraid to marry for the second time," he advised. "Second marriages seem to work out quite well." But he added this note of caution: If you are going to get married for the second time, think it out. It may be much more difficult than your first marriage. Work out some of the bugs before saying "I do."

"If there are going to be children involved," Schlesinger counseled, "get them involved in the second marriage as much as possible and help them understand what this means, so that when they enter a second marriage, they at least are involved in it in a meaningful way. These are generalities, of course, but they may be of help to those who are thinking of marrying for the second time."

Schlesinger has written widely on the subject. Not long

ago he commented in *Family Life*, published by the American Institute of Family Relations, that "remarriage is an art in itself. It means a depth of self-understanding never before achieved, an insight into the past, with an eye to the future, a maturity of thought and of reason far beyond that which is minimum.

"It is its own form of therapy, since the problems brought to it are settled by it, although new ones continually arise. It is now two people, not one; two minds, not one; you are no longer alone. Remarriage shows a strength of character and a belief in oneself that surprises all of us; it shows a discarding of all the fears of making another mistake—a new start on a new road—whether widowed or divorced. Every day starts another chapter in a continuing life story. To be able to accept the visiting natural mother or father without strain is a great deal to ask; to do so is a sign of wisdom and maturity, or a realization of the facts of life as they are.

"It is important to keep the family together as much as possible, regardless of outside influences. These are the signs of understanding, of tolerance, of a deep and abiding faith in what is right. Whether your new children call you Mom or Dad, or any other name that is comfortable to them—this is not important. It is important that the acceptance be complete, on both sides. Everything else will follow in time, and with patience."

Some children of the widowed try to throw up obstacles to remarriage. They may expect their parents to live in celibacy in honor of the deceased. They may fear that a new marriage will threaten their relationship with their parents or that they will be cut off from their share of the family estate. Quite a few children, even those who are themselves mature, are convinced that their aging parents have had no sex life, so they wonder why in the world Mother would want to get married again.

Once the decision to get married is made, the legal

matters have been attended to, and the wedding plans have been fixed, a kind of serenity settles on a good many middle-agers. There is much more than a difference in age between young and aging couples, according to a man who observes hundreds every year. Thomas Lennane, the first deputy clerk of the New York City Marriage License Bureau, has noticed an air of contentment and an absence of awkwardness in older couples, while the younger ones tend to be nervous. Although the young couples are often accompanied by friends or relatives, older prospective brides and bridegrooms turn up by themselves and seem to be more at ease as they fill out the forms.

"I would honestly say that the older bride—and the groom—appear a little bit more settled, perhaps even less nervous—seem to be more content—in a quieter frame of mind than the younger brides coming in," Lennane said.

Bridal consultants for large department stores concur. They find the mature bride remaining calm and usually shopping for a dress she can wear again, in a color rather than white. Few older brides want formal weddings with all the trimmings.

"The older bride is not as bubbly and excited as the teen-ager," a wedding consultant observed. "She's more practical. Also, she's better looking than you'd expect. Sometimes I'm surprised when I find out how old the bride is. I guess hormones have something to do with it, but forty-five year olds today look like what I would call thirty year olds."

CHAPTER
7

Out to Work: Be Back After Sixty-five

THE DOCTOR listened sympathetically to Mrs. Pollifax when she told him she was bored with volunteer work and her life as a widow. She felt she had outlived her usefulness in her present way of life, and she seemed to be downright disappointed at the news that her health was satisfactory. Then she confided in the young physician that what she needed was a new lease on life. She wanted to be a spy!

He laughed at her, but as anyone knows who read the best-selling suspense novel *The Unexpected Mrs. Pollifax*, or saw the movie starring Rosalind Russell, Mrs. Pollifax did indeed become a spy—and a daring one. Except for the fact that she took up espionage as her "golden age" activity, the conversation in the doctor's office surely has been duplicated countless times in real life. The fictional doctor laughed at Mrs. Pollifax when she disclosed her secret ambition, and there are those who probably would find humor in many of the things older women do or want to do; but more and more grandmothers are putting rocking chairs farther into their futures and getting out into the world, working at everything from digging graves and driving taxis to becoming executives. Some work part time, some full time, but like Mrs. Pollifax, they find remunerative activity more fulfilling than forcing themselves to smile over often-menial volunteer tasks.

"I can shovel with anybody," declared Mrs. Vella Armstrong of Argyle, Wisconsin, a grandmother who has been gainfully employed as a gravedigger since 1960. In addition to wielding a pick, shovel, crowbar, grub hoe, wedge, and ax to dig graves at eight cemeteries, she mows the lawn at one of them. "A woman really ain't made for it," she declares, "but I've worked hard all my life. I used to walk behind a walking plow, and that was hard, too."

For Mrs. Gloria Honacker, a divorcée with five children, driving a New York taxicab for more than ten years has been her answer, not only financially but psychologically. "There's no better job," she maintains, "but you have to like to drive. You have so much freedom, and you feel like you're your own boss. I don't think I could ever go back to being a waitress again." So devoted is Mrs. Honacker to her work that she joined a foreign-affairs class at the United Nations so she could talk more intelligently with the diplomats who ride in her cab. Another middle-aged cabby, Mrs. Ella Sheppard, who dons the latest fashions for her hours behind the wheel, works part time to supplement her husband's income as a warehouseman. Mrs. Mary McLaughlin, the mother of six, started hacking at the suggestion of her doctor, who thought it would calm her nerves. "He was right," she admits. "It cured me of my nerves. Now nothing bothers me." That was nearly fifteen years ago, and in the interval, she has delivered two babies in her cab, fought off two would-be muggers, and rescued an elderly couple from a building that burst into flames as she drove by.

A more sheltered and sedate occupation was sought by

Mrs. Grace Shea, the grandmother of six, when she entered part-time office work at the age of seventy. She had been a United States Navy supervisor for twenty years, with a total of twenty-eight years in federal service, until her mandatory retirement at sixty-five. Because of her knowledge and skills, the Navy rehired her, and she remained on the job until an economy wave caught up with her on her seventieth birthday and she was retired again.

"I stayed home a year," she recalls. "Then I began to feel I wasn't enough a part of anything. It gave me a terribly let-down feeling."

Mrs. Shea had no typing or stenographic skills, which made finding a job difficult, but she did have considerable knowledge of office procedure, which enabled her to get the part-time job she wanted. "You can get a job without knowing typing if you're willing to file, sort, collate, address envelopes or cards, or keep a few simple records," she says. But before finding her position with the American Girl Service, she worked as a temporary office worker, addressing Christmas cards for a bachelor and helping him with his gift planning so efficiently that she worked as his social secretary for a time after that. This led to other temporary jobs, which made it possible for her to work as much or as little as she wished in order to supplement her retirement income. "We have to overcome older people's impressions that they can't find jobs," Mrs. Shea believes. "When I report for work, no one ever asks my age. They take me at face value."

Even if a woman works only for spending money, it is time well invested, for it may keep her from having to be a pinchpenny or enable her to take an occasional trip, as does one woman we know who works nine months every year and travels in Europe the other three.

There are all kinds of opportunities for work—interesting work—for older women. For example, Mimi Randolph, a retired character actress, became the first woman floor clerk on the New York Cotton Exchange at a point well beyond middle age. After Mrs. Julie Rich went back to work at forty-plus, so many people asked her how they could do it, too, that she made a career of a "Back to Careers Program" to prepare women for jobs in their mature years. Mrs. Rich originally took the volunteer route back to becoming involved, serving as publicity chairman for a number of organizations before becoming assistant director of advertising for the Garden State Plaza Shopping Center in Paramus, New Jersey. Because shopping centers are becoming more and more community oriented, she decided to develop a program for women of the area, starting with a fashion show to help the older ones find the right clothes. Then she branched out into seminars in which representatives of business, education, and industry advised women on how they could get back to work. In the process Mrs. Rich learned that the biggest stumbling block for most women is their lack of self-confidence. They think nobody wants them after forty. That is not so, Mrs. Rich contends. "My kids tell me I'm a pretty swinging mom," she boasts.

Another middle-ager who is "with it" is Candy Jones, the mother of two grown sons and one of the famous cover girls of the 1950s, who now trains and grooms women of all ages so that they can begin modeling careers or so they can function at top form at whatever they are doing. She finds a demand for mature, matronly models to display clothes appropriate for the middle-aged and to appear at trade shows to demonstrate products used by women. "The older woman is more believable," Miss Jones says. "She's not going to try to put across to the public the notion that it is the nineteen-or-twenty-year-old girl who is doing the housework or the cooking." One woman Miss Jones represents is a widow in her seventies who left Ohio for New York because she needed to earn money and could not get work in her hometown. She began as a chambermaid in a hotel off Fifth Avenue to raise cash for the proper attire to wear for a job interview, including a wig. Now that she is doing nicely as a model and has managed to save her family's old homestead in Ohio, she wants to stay in New York and keep on working.

Direct selling is a popular field among the mature. Mrs. Helen Beyers, a Harrisburg, Pennsylvania, grandmother who never made more than $125 a week in her years as a seamstress, found her niche as a sales representative, and now banks an income well into six figures as a divisional organizer for Princess House, a direct-selling party-plan company. She serves as a leader for nearly eleven hundred women in five eastern states, many of whom have been earning high five-figure incomes. Most are middle-aged and able to set their own working hours, so they have plenty of time for home and family and whatever else they want to do.

Another Princess House success story is that of Mrs. Barbara Mae Myers, who found her key to a happy "retirement" in direct selling. When she retired from her job as an accounting technician with the state of California in Sacramento, she had already started her new career during her spare time. As a result, when she put away her ledgers, she was well into her Princess House order pad. It was not long before she was promoted to the key position of area organizer, recruiting and training other women to show and sell Princess House merchandise. At the age of forty-two she had reared six children and had three grandchildren. In addition to her work with Princess House, she still had plenty of time for her favorite pastimes of cake decorating, crocheting, and handicrafts.

All four thousand of the representatives selling for Princess House are women, and a woman serves as vice-president in charge of sales. She is Mrs. Adelaide ("Dee") Rossi, who helped found the company in a rented converted chicken coop in Rehoboth, Massachusetts. Mrs. Rossi was nearing forty when she entered direct selling after reading a classified advertisement in her local newspaper saying "no experience necessary." It sought a woman willing to be trained from the ground up for an executive position. Mrs. Rossi recalls that she could scarcely believe her eyes. Her experience had been as an archivist in the United States Embassy in Lima, Peru, as an airline employee, as a telephone company business representative, and, most recently, as a wife and the mother of two.

As her son and daughter grew older she took stock of herself and decided that she wanted to go back to work, into something in which she had no background, something that would really be a challenge. "I had gotten to the stage of life where I thought all I was doing was chasing dirt and running after children," she says. "I wanted something completely different." If she was going to have some kind of meaningful career, she told herself, she had better get started, because she feared that "after forty nobody would take me." That led her to the classified section of the Providence *Journal* and the career she was looking for. The career eventually became Princess House and active participation in the building of one of the most successful and fastest-growing direct-selling companies in the country. By answering the ad Mrs. Rossi not only changed the course of her own life but, as time went on, she helped many other women find careers in the business world.

Direct selling has provided a route to financial security and psychological health for thousands of women in middle age and beyond. It is work anyone can do, and sometimes the shyest, most reserved women turn out to be the most successful.

A FUTURE FOR WOMEN WHO HAVE NEVER WORKED

We read almost every day about women who have succeeded in the professions and business. Most have worked all their lives and are being rewarded at last for their diligence in their second forties. Our concern here is to try to open some doors for the middle-aged woman who has *never* worked, who has not worked for a number of years, or who wants a different kind of job in her retirement. Mrs. Lois Gray of Lee's Summit, Missouri, provides us with an example of a successful older woman who got her start in middle age. Now in her seventies, Mrs. Gray is the all-time top sales representative for a national financial-services complex with headquarters in Kansas City. She joined the firm in 1949, after a middle-age divorce left her as her family's breadwinner; since then, she has sold more than $20 million in mutual funds, forging to the lead of the three thousand other members of the company's sales force. What is more, 70 per cent of her customers are men. "I have never 'turned on the charm' or taken advantage of the fact that I am a woman in trying to sell a male prospect," she said. Working a seven-day week, Mrs. Gray spurns the idea of retirement, declaring, "I intend to wear out, not rust out."

Employers are becoming increasingly aware that the Mrs. Grays of the world tend to make good workers. Their attendance record is likely to be better than that of younger women. They are more conscientious in their efforts to do a good job, and they are not there to "prove" anything except that they can be productive. Executives are bending a little more in their approach to the woman worker as a result of such diligence. Some are becoming less rigid about requiring that office staffs put in a nine-to-five day, finding that mothers and grandmothers can increase a firm's efficiency and production if they are allowed to set their hours to fit their schedules at home. Rather than hiring one younger woman who is there just to fill the hours and collect a paycheck, some businesses have set up a schedule whereby they hire two older people who split each workday. The productivity that has resulted has amazed some personnel officers and has led a prominent St. Louis businessman, Lisle M. Ramsey, to the conclusion that women are the greatest untapped natural resource in the country. Ramsey has promoted women into key positions on the home office staff of his company, which franchises photography studios, nearly all of which are operated by women, mainly middle-agers.

Dr. Esther Westervelt, director of research for the New York State Guidance Center for Women and former adjunct associate professor of guidance and higher education at Teachers College of Columbia University, agrees with Ramsey but expresses her view in a slightly different way: "American women comprise the largest leisure class that has ever been known. They are able to fill their lives with busywork, and it is empty." Dr. Westervelt says that working outside the home adds new dimensions to the identities of women who are lonely and bored and need more activity and association with more people. "Home can be a very lonely place today," she observed, "and the people one meets within it or within the neighborhood can tend over the years to provide rather monotonous conversational fare."

Speaking directly from the experience of having hired a number of women past forty, a few in their sixties, Mrs. Dorothy Roy, director of personnel for the Hearthstone Insurance Company of Massachusetts, said her firm has found older women to be the most conscientious workers. "I think they are better housekeepers," she said. "The older women we hired worked first in our file area, where you have to be a good housekeeper. Their files were kept so well you could find anything."

With the installation of computers to do most of the filing, Hearthstone reassigned the women to other departments, where they function as well as, or better than before, and in more sophisticated jobs. Most had never worked in an office before, but some had been department store clerks or had held factory jobs. Those who had never been employed had found themselves with little to do after their children were grown. "Many were going through the change," Mrs. Roy said. "Their doctors told them to get out of the house. I think that some of them went to work as an escape or as therapy. They are really great. The office situation has replaced their family life. This may be dime-store psychology, but it would appear that way. They have little parties when somebody has a birthday. They make a big deal out of birthdays or a new baby. If you ever want to taste the best cooking in the world, go to one of their birthday parties. They knock themselves out to see who is going to bring the best dish, the best cake, the best cookies. I think they've just substituted the office for their home."

Perhaps one or two of the score or more women over forty who were hired by Hearthstone sought work out of economic necessity. Mrs. Roy has found that most came primarily for something to do. One woman told Mrs. Roy that on weekends she could hardly wait for Monday morning so she could go back to work. "Her friends who are at home all day bore her now, even though the job she is doing is very repetitive; you could almost call it monotonous," Mrs. Roy added. "But she's exposed to all sorts of bright young people at work, and she, like others, dresses more stylishly and wears younger clothes because she can see what younger women are wearing."

The advantages to the company are many, Mrs. Roy finds. There is less absenteeism among the older workers.

They are more punctual. And, she added, they care more about the product.

On the negative side, some men are reluctant to supervise the work of older women, probably because they subconsciously feel as if they are telling their mothers what to do. As far as the older woman herself is concerned, she tends to take a possessive attitude toward her work. Mrs. Roy attributes this to her having become used to being at home, where she thought in terms of "my" and "mine." "When they come to work, it's the same thing," Mrs. Roy noted. "This is '*my* drawer,' '*my* file,' and 'these are *my* papers.' Another negative, I think, is that older women don't adapt as easily as young ones. You can't move them from one job to another as easily as you can a young person. Somebody sat on a yellow chair yesterday, and you've given them a green chair today. This kind of thing causes some of them to rebel."

However, Mrs. Roy feels that it is possible to help women overcome such inflexibility, and she also finds a positive aspect to it, for "if it is *theirs,* they want it to be the best, so I think you are getting the best although it has a little tint of negativeness."

One woman in her middle years sits quietly at her desk in Hearthstone's home office in Brookline, Massachusetts, and does more work in a day than a younger person might do in two or three, despite the fact that she has the tedious job of filing insurance policies numerically, which requires good eyesight and the kind of "sitability" younger people do not have. "These women are successful," Mrs. Roy said, "because I think the younger women want a lot more activity. They want to be jumping from one thing to another. The woman over forty is very happy to have a sit-down job."

Hearthstone, like its parent company, the Combined Insurance Company of America, has found that its policy of nondiscrimination because of age has paid off in reduced turnover among the older workers. Older employees, men as well as women, are more likely to take advantage of the company's profit-sharing plan, which provides retirement security, and also of other benefits, including health and accident protection. You can hear a pin drop when you walk into a room in which a number of older women are working. At first this surprised some of the men on the staff, who could not imagine twenty or more women in one room without a constant flow of chatter.

"I would say that as a group they have no pressing problems, as far as we are concerned," Mrs. Roy commented. "Whatever problems they have are very minor. They are dedicated. Having been loyal to a family for twenty or twenty-five years, they carry their loyalty with them to work. A young girl has no loyalties except to her own activity and her own interest."

One of the older women Mrs. Roy hired is a former dancing teacher in her fifties who was employed by Hearthstone to work in a clerical capacity in its customer-service department. When it came time for the company's annual Christmas party, she asked for permission to stage a show and offered to handle the entire production. "I wish you could have seen that gal dance," Mrs. Roy recalled. "She took a group of kids who didn't know their right foot from their left and put them in a Rockettes line. They were tremendous.

"Not long ago, she told me that this job had saved her because she had lost her husband and had gone through all sorts of things. She knew she couldn't have a dancing school eight hours a day the way she used to. She had never been in business before. I think this work for her *really* was a lifesaver. In preparing for the Christmas show, she was in there pitching every night, teaching routines, all on her own time. She went the extra mile—and she had a marvelous time doing it."

SOME THOUGHTS ON SUPPLEMENTARY INCOME

Many retired people find they *need* to work part-time or engage in businesses that require only a few hours a day to supplement their other income. Under the Social Security program, a person is limited in how much he can earn a year in a job or in his own business; otherwise he will lose part or all of his benefits. The maximum allowable income is woefully small, but Congress is chipping away at the ceiling and may someday arrive at a realistic figure. There is one bright side to this picture, for the holdouts, at age seventy-two, can work full time and still draw a full Social Security allowance. It takes plenty of perseverance and stamina to do this, however.

Part-time work is particularly appealing to older women who have never held jobs before. As we have pointed out, more and more companies are hiring part-time help, and older people are being more widely accepted for these jobs. Private employment agencies are opening their doors to people who want only part-time retirement. One of these is Mature Temps, Inc., an agency sponsored by the American Association of Retired Persons, which maintains offices in nine major cities to help older citizens find productive part-time employment, mainly clerical. State employment offices in some of the larger cities have established experimental Older Worker Service Units under the United States Employment Service, providing counseling and job placement without charge. There are also Federal Job Information Centers that keep older people apprised of openings in about seventy cities. Other agencies offering assistance are Foster Grandparents, operated by the Administration on the Aging; Green Thumb and Green Light, created by the National Farmers Union under a grant from the Department of Labor; Volunteers in Service to America (VISTA); and the Teachers Corps. Before the Nixon administration started phasing out the Peace Corps, a number of older people had been accepted for assignments in foreign countries.

One woman who helped us type an early draft of this manuscript was employed as a "regular temporary." At the age of seventy she was receiving regular Social Security benefits but worked a few hours a day, just enough to earn the maximum allowable. She selected the days and hours most convenient for her; on completion of the job, she used her part-time earnings to take a trip. When she returned, we were able to use her services for another task. This is the way many women operate, making themselves available as needed in offices during peak production periods, and we can vouch for the fact that those who follow this procedure are dependable and hardworking.

To carry our own experience a step further, the final manuscript was typed by a chic young grandmother who had worked before her marriage but remained at home while her children were growing up. Now that she no longer has as many responsibilities, she likes to work part time, both to keep active and to take home a little extra money.

For those who prefer to work for themselves, operating a part-time small business offers many advantages. A self-employed woman can set her own pace and have the satisfaction of being more creative than would be the case if she worked for someone else. It should be noted that many small businesses require a certain amount of capital and financial know-how, and that, generally speaking, retirement is not the time to invest one's life savings in starting a business, for the risks are too great. In direct selling, however, as we have indicated, there are many opportunities for a woman to be her own boss with little or no cash outlay required to get started. The Direct-

Selling Association has a list of reputable concerns that are always looking for women to sell for them, and those interested in pursuing this line can write to it at 1730 M Street, NW, Washington, D.C. 20036.

According to a *Good Housekeeping* poll, 75 per cent of all mothers have had part-time or full-time jobs. Doing what? Here is a partial list of occupations:

- Baby-sitter
- Bank clerk or teller
- Beautician
- Bookbinder
- Car hop
- Camp counselor
- Cashier
- Caterer
- Comparison shopper
- Cosmetologist
- Court reporter
- Credit investigator
- Day-care nursery attendant
- Decorator
- Demonstrator of toys, cosmetics, clothing, jewelry, or food
- Dental assistant
- Dietician
- Direct saleswoman
- Florist
- Greenhouse assistant
- Hotel clerk
- Insurance agent
- Laboratory assistant
- Librarian
- Manicurist
- Market researcher
- Medical assistant
- Model
- Mutual-fund saleswoman
- Nurse's aide
- Office worker
- Photographer
- Practical nurse
- Proofreader
- Real estate agent
- Receptionist
- Relief switchboard operator
- Rental agent
- Saleswoman
- School aide
- School bus driver
- School-crossing guard
- Seamstress
- Secretary
- Sewing machine operator
- Telephone operator
- Teletypist
- Ticket seller
- Travel agent
- Typist
- Waitress
- X-ray technician

Some of this work can be done at home. Other ways of earning money without leaving home include catering, taking care of children and pets, sewing, and operating a roadside stand.

WHAT IT TAKES TO GET AHEAD IN BUSINESS

Success in running your own business requires many attributes, according to Guin Hall, a former newspaperwoman who later served as deputy commissioner of the now-discontinued Woman's Program of the New York State Department of Commerce. "You have to have talent," she says. "You have to have something to sell, whether it's a service or product, that is needed in your particular area, and you have to be able to do it well. You also have to have the money to do it well, and not rely on the income for anywhere from a year to five years." She also notes that every successful businesswoman that she has interviewed acknowledged that if she had realized how much was going to be involved in hardship, energy, and time, she probably would never have accepted the challenge. At the same time, the women Miss Hall talked with indicated that they were glad they had started their own business and had attained satisfaction from their success.

If a woman is determined to launch her own part-time business, Miss Hall recommends that she look for a need to be filled, because there is always room for one more service organization in any community. Many skills, such as repairing lampshades, are no longer widely practiced, so a woman with such a talent may find she has more work than she can handle. Businesses operated by women naturally tend to involve feminine interests in fashions, food, sewing, home decorating, and related fields. There is no reason, as far as Miss Hall is concerned, that women should limit themselves to such pursuits, for a wide range of opportunities lies before them. The trick is to try to develop whatever talents you possess and then put them to work.

Ruth Weil, although far from retirement, has set an example others might seek to follow. She turned her interest in people and their problems into a successful personal shopping service in New York City. Through Le Shopping, she buys a wide variety of items for her customers, whether it be an inexpensive cheese wedge rolled in walnuts or a high-priced Wedgewood telephone cover. "I'm enchanted by people," she told us, "and having my own business gives me contact with all kinds of people whom I might not be meeting if I were sitting in a business office having a routine kind of career."

Most cities have business advisory services to provide information for people seeking to develop their own enterprises. The Small Business Administration in Washington, D.C., has a list of these and can send you the address of the one nearest you. (Write to the Administration at 1441 L Street N.W., Washington, D.C. 20416.) Meanwhile, it might be a good idea to take a business education course at a night school and look around to see what services there are in your community—and which are needed. Or go to work part time in a business you like and learn how it operates before you branch out on your own.

In *Back to Work, Ladies,* a career guide for the mature woman by Toni Stollenwerk (Pilot Books, 347 Fifth Avenue, New York City 10016, 1967), she advises a middle-aged job seeker to think about the work she has performed in the home. "As a supermarket shopper, you would probably put many a purchasing agent to shame. Despite all the kidding we gals take about balancing our checkbooks, statistics show that women handle the family finances in many more homes than we ever dared suspect. Weren't there times when coming out even with your budget required so much juggling and planning that you were sure the Senate Finance Committee could not do better?"

SOME ADVICE FROM THE EXPERTS

When you consider that 43 per cent of American women are in the labor force today, as compared with only 23 per cent in 1920, and that the average woman worker is married and thirty-nine years old (in 1920 she was single and twenty-eight), it is obvious that opportunities for the older woman are expanding. But if statistics are not enough to convince you, read what experts in the employment field have to say.

"I think it's quite unfair to discriminate against women or men because of age," declared Elmer Winter, president of Manpower, Inc., of Milwaukee, in an interview. "I really think it's the abilities and not the anniversaries that should apply in the hiring of people.

"Some people can be old at thirty-five. Some aren't old until they're sixty or sixty-five. We've hired many, many women in their fifties and sixties and we really have had experience with people in that age group. Now, some will not do well, but certainly the great preponderance of people who work for us in those age areas do a very fine job."

Mr. Winter finds that the mature woman who comes to him is most likely to be skilled in secretarial work, stenography, or typing, in that order. He has no trouble placing a woman with any of these skills; calls no longer come very often from employers saying, "Don't send me anybody over thirty-five." If a personnel director objects, Mr. Winter tries to talk him into at least giving a qualified woman over forty a chance. When he succeeds in doing this, he invariably gets a report that "she is great!"

"Many women who come to work for us are a little

nervous," Mr. Winter observed, "a little unsure of their skills. They don't know whether they can make it in the world of work, and a temporary assignment gives them an opportunity to regain their confidence. Many people like to change around. One day, or one week, they might enjoy being in an advertising agency; the next week they're working in an insurance company or at a TV station. To be on temporary assignments gives them an opportunity to really get out and see what makes business tick and meet new people."

Women who have been wives and mothers for years may feel, without cause, that they do not know where to fit in, that they do not have any marketable skills, but Mr. Winter says that by keeping records for the PTA or the church guild, a woman develops a skill for clerical work. "A woman with a nice, warm, outgoing personality can get a job as a demonstrator," he said. Thousands of unskilled women with something more than outgoing personalities to recommend them are employed as demonstrators in supermarkets. Telephone surveys and solicitations keep many women busy at home, and there is a desperate need in industry for people without skills who are willing to learn.

Sabatino A. Russo, Jr., president and founder of American Girl Service, which has sixty offices that find temporary work for twenty thousand women a year, is another who stands foursquare behind Mom on the job. "The place of the mature woman today is back working," he is convinced. "So many of them have magnificent skills and abilities and they find that they feel that they are not wanted and are over the hill. The fact is that they are not, that their skills are needed in industry and by firms like ours." Not only are the number of unfilled jobs reaching what Mr. Russo terms "incredible" proportions, but studies made in the last few years show that employers often prefer the mature woman.

When American Girl Service made a vigorous effort to recruit mature women, it found that they not only were available but were skilled and responsible, did not get involved in office politics, performed a workmanlike job —and were not using the boss's time to look for husbands. Another attribute of the "retread" is that she is likely to have a better education than the younger woman. Unfortunately, however, many middle-agers are unwilling to start at the bottom in an office job, thinking that they have served their apprenticeship at home raising a family, so they may reject the idea of work unless they can be managers. Those women find it difficult to accept the fact that they cannot start where they left off when they "retired" to motherhood twenty years earlier. At the same time, a woman is "out of her mind," as far as Mr. Russo is concerned, if, before she gets married, she does not prepare herself for a job in the event of widowhood or other economic necessity. And she should maintain whatever skills she has in case of an emergency and not simply give up.

To help women overcome the "lack of confidence crisis," Mr. Russo's organization conducted symposiums to make them feel better about themselves and let them know that companies really wanted them. After the ice was broken, employers began to ask for older women. Although an occasional woman develops severe emotional problems in the menopause, Mr. Russo said, usually "work is a great therapy for a woman because it keeps her active and her mind busy. She's creating, producing, getting a sense of her own worth." Work becomes her best medicine; it gives a new outlook on life. Those who entered the world of work with trepidation and fear of failure develop a new sense of self, which leads Mr. Russo to the conclusion that "the mature woman owes herself the obligation to use her skills. She owes the country that obligation and she certainly owes society that obligation.

I don't think there is anything more valuable to a woman or more self-fulfilling than to collect a paycheck at the end of the week, because that is a measure of a person's worth." He added that while volunteer work is wonderful and can provide experience for a paying job, there is nothing more satisfying than a paycheck, even a small one. "The best advice I can give would be to say that the world is your oyster, but before you can do anything about it, you have got to open the shell. The way to open the shell is to do something about going back to work and make up your mind to diligently seek it and not be disappointed or discouraged if the first time you go out to look for work for some reason or other you are turned down or there just isn't an opening. Try again and organize that search."

LET'S HEAR FROM SOME WOMEN WHO HAVE BEEN THERE

"There is only one way to return to work, and that is to make it your own decision. Don't go about asking people—your friends, your relatives, even your children—for permission or assurance that it is all right to go back to work. Only you can know your needs and determination. When you ask for advice, ask it of professionals."

Those were strong words—and words that did not jibe with what we heard from some others—but they came from a woman who had been there herself, Sara Welles Briller, who has worked all her adult life and has shared the fruits of her experience in her book *Born Female,* written with Caroline Bird.

In an interview, Mrs. Briller warned the middle-aged retread that she should not kid herself into thinking she can move from the kitchen into an executive job. "Be realistic," she admonished. "Don't expect to fly up there easily to the top. I don't mean that you should forget about advancement, that you should give up ambitions, or that you should pretend about it. I do mean that women need to know a lot more about their own histories, about their own situations socially."

She spoke, too, about the assumption many men falsely make that women are more emotional on the job and that menopause makes them particularly difficult. "Any woman who has worked for any length of time in important positions with men, closely involved with the decisions that they have to make, can tell you how false that is," she said. "Men lose their tempers, as a matter of fact, more often than women, and yet when a man loses his temper on the job, people think he is just proving his interest in his work. When a woman loses her temper, she is regarded as 'being emotional.'"

Writing in the March 1970 issue of *The Woman Physician*, Dr. Mathilda R. Vaschak, director of medical services for E. R. Squibb & Sons, Inc., noted in a discussion, "The Mature Woman in Industry," that several decades ago there was considerable concern about the menopausal woman, who was considered to be mercurial and to have a high absentee rate. Some executives of those days felt that older women were unable to adapt themselves to pressures for higher productivity or to be motivated by a desire on the part of management for higher profits. Dr. Vaschak noted, however, that older women have shown a strong motivation and a keen desire to use their education and skills in work they consider to be important. The mature woman is more often interested in what she is doing for its own values, and therefore is far more likely to report regularly for work—and on time—than a younger woman, according to Dr. Vaschak. But she added that the mature woman needs to be appreciated, and this may be her principal motivation on the job.

HOW TO GO ABOUT GETTING A JOB

Persistence probably is the key ingredient to reentering the business world. Don't be surprised if your first job application is turned down—and don't be discouraged if it happens five or six times. There *is* a job for you, but you will have to look for it, perhaps for quite a while. Statistics indicate that it usually takes a middle-aged woman longer than a younger woman to get a satisfactory job, but once she lands it, she is likely to remain in it for as long as she wants to work—and to enjoy it.

Here are several things you might consider:

—Be sure that you *really* want to go to work, in fairness to yourself, your family, and your employers.

—If possible, try to obtain the support and approval of your family before you get a job. If they are resistant, however, you do not have to give in to them. Look around for something to do, and when you have found it, tell the family that you are about to embark on a new activity outside the home that will open up new horizons for you and will make you more interesting to yourself, and to them, and also bring in added income. Don't be defensive about it. Take a positive stance. Other women who have done this have become so successful that their families have admitted they were wrong in their opposition.

—Make a list of your assets—education, training you have had since you left school, your favorite subjects when you were a student, and the kind of student you were.

—Make a list of your work experience and skills. Can you type, and how fast? What volunteer jobs have you done? What are your hobbies? Have you helped your husband in his business? Skills have been required in all of these things. What are *your* skills?

—Analyze the kind of person you are. Are you neat, punctual, receptive to criticism, able to concentrate? Do you get along with others, especially those younger than you? Are you flexible? How is your health? Do you work best with your hands or your head? How are your human relations? Are you willing and able to learn new things?

Now that you have listed your assets, what about your liabilities, your limitations?

—When you went to school, what were the subjects you liked least and did the poorest in? Can you see any gaps in your knowledge that would limit your ability? Do you tend to dwell on shortcomings?

—In considering your work experience, in or out of the home, what did you like and dislike and what did you do well or poorly?

—Getting down to the real you, ask yourself these questions. "Can I stand on my feet all day?" "Do I mind noise or crowded offices?" "Can I take pressure?" "Would I object to working with and for women?" "How would I react to working with men? Could I forget I am a woman and yet still act like one?"

—What are the hours and days you would be available for work and what length vacation would you need?

Taking into consideration what you have included in both of your lists, now make still another list of the jobs for which you feel your experience would best qualify you. Don't stop at one or two items. Jot down every possible job to which your interests, experience, and ability might lead you. Ask yourself also: "What would I like most to do?"

Now you are almost ready to look for a job, but there is one more thing you need to learn to do: prepare a résumé to leave with your prospective employer.

The secret of a good résumé is to make it brief and to the point, without embellishment; it should be typed, with your name, address, and telephone number in the upper left-hand corner. In the upper right, indicate the kind of work you want. Then on the body of the page concisely list biographical information, remembering that it is not necessary to state your birth date, although you may if you wish. If you note your place of birth, education, marital status, number of children, and experience, the prospective employer will get an idea of how "mature" you are. Under education include schools, the dates you attended, whether you graduated, and your major interests. Also include any education you have had since leaving school.

When it comes to job experience, list your last three or four assignments, in reverse order, starting with the most recent. Include the name, address, and telephone number of your employers, dates of employment, name and title of your supervisors, and a brief description of the work you performed.

List volunteer activities, including names, addresses, and telephone numbers, the dates (again in reverse order), type of service, and the name and address of an official who is familiar with your work.

Add two or three personal reference, with names, addresses, telephone numbers, and positions of the individuals involved.

If you have been a housewife for the last twenty years, do not panic while preparing a résumé. State that fact frankly, but also include your volunteer involvements and the skills you have acquired as a homemaker.

When you start looking for work, tell everyone you can what you are doing. Visit the local employment service, read the classified ads, call on employment agencies, and check major employers in your area, getting their names out of the classified telephone directory, from the chamber of commerce, or city or county personnel offices. Call on hospitals, schools, unions, professional associations, nonprofit agencies. Tell all of them of your availability. And you can also advertise in the local newspaper.

After doing all of these things, you are ready for an interview, probably the most critical step in the job-finding process. Learn everything you can about a business or organization before you make an appointment—its background, products or services, number of employees, etc. Dress neatly and appropriately; if you normally use glasses or a hearing aid, wear them to the interview. Be prompt, and if you have to wait in an anteroom, try to appear alert. Look over any reading matter on display and give the impression that you are happy to be there. You should have with you your résumé and Social Security number and a notebook for jotting down any information you need. Try to appear self-confident, but not overconfident, and assume a positive attitude. Leave your problems at home; don't give a prospective employer a hard-luck story or too many details about your life. In other words, don't talk too much. Respond with interest and enthusiasm, and by all means be frank and brief, and don't be timid about asking questions about the company and the work. If you are given an application form, fill it out completely and legibly, being sure to read every question carefully first.

As the conversation closes, tell the interviewer how much you appreciate his having taken time to see you and that you hope to hear from him soon.

And—keep on looking. Give yourself a choice if you possibly can; you will be less likely to encounter disappointment and more likely to find the job that is right for you.

THE EDUCATIONAL ROUTE TO EMPLOYMENT

What has come to be known as continuing education, but in actuality may be more a resumption of education, has provided an avenue leading to careers in middle age for many women. There are training opportunities in high schools, junior colleges, colleges, and universities, in federal agencies, in private business, and in trade and technical schools as well as through correspondence courses and television study. Middle-aged women are going back to school to become registered or practical nurses or laboratory assistants, dietitians or assistants in doctors' offices. Of the seven hundred classifications of jobs in hospitals, a good number are tailored for the mature woman. There are opportunities for education to become administrators of cultural resources such as art galleries, theater workshops, community music projects, and urban community development activities.

Bertha Stronach, former international president of the National Secretaries Association and administrator of International Business Machines' educational training programs, emphasizes that there is a shortage of secretarial help and the job market is good, particularly for the more mature woman. "Management has found that the mature woman can assume a great deal more responsibility with a calmer attitude and a greater sense of responsibility," she told us. "If she has had previous secretarial experience, she does need some type of brushup, because she may feel a little out of date, a little out of style, a little out of practice. If she has never had secretarial training and wants to come back into the office, she should take some type of intensive training course at a business school or college. Being a secretary—and a good one—will give you a much better insight into what is needed in business, and it will open many doors to you that might otherwise be closed."

One of the largest programs that prepare mature women for careers is conducted by the Council for Continuing Education of Women of Greater Miami, a department of the downtown campus of Miami Dade Junior College. The center offers information and referrals for women and guides them to schools where they can resume their educations. In its My Fair Lady Program, the council has interviewed hundreds of women since it opened in 1966, and at any given time has eight hundred to fifteen hundred enrolled in courses ranging from technical subjects to what are called "rusty lady seminars," an eight-lecture series. The idea, says Betty Kaynor, the coordinator, is to "keep our brains going."

Mrs. Kaynor entered the program as a "rusty lady" volunteer after twenty years as an active Junior Leaguer in her home town of Waterbury, Connecticut, and then in Miami. For a while she had worked part time for the college, using the knowledge she had acquired while living abroad during the years her husband served as an international development specialist. When she applied for a job as an adviser to foreign students, she was told they did not have a place for her on the payroll but asked her to serve as a volunteer in the new program for women. After six months of working for nothing, Mrs. Kaynor, a college graduate with a major in psychology, was put on the payroll part time. Now she is a full-time faculty member of Dade Junior College, with a number of stories to tell about the results of the My Fair Lady Program. One woman had thought that at fifty-seven she would never get a job. Then she enrolled in a "rusty lady" seminar, which led her to training in retail sales and a job in a local department store where she soon was promoted to assistant manager of the women's ready-to-wear department. Another woman, who worked as a public school cafeteria aide to help support her family, appeared at a seminar in a Girl Scout uniform. Noting that she must have a talent for working with children, Mrs. Kaynor encouraged her to return to school and she subsequently became a kindergarten teacher.

What Mrs. Kaynor regards as her classic case is that of Clara Shone, "our fisherlady." Mrs. Shone read a newspaper story about the Miami program and wrote from Marathon, Florida, where she was working as captain of her own fishing boat. A widow, she was worried about having to spend too much time away from her ten-year-old daughter. She had been writing stories about Sammy and Sally Sailfish, was a dedicated conservationist, and wanted to remain near the sea. At Mrs. Kaynor's urging, Mrs. Shone took two semesters of a hotel-keeping course and returned to Marathon, where she became head housekeeper at a large beach motel, which gave her free housing, good wages, and a chance to keep her child with her.

By this time Mrs. Shone was hooked on going to school. She proceeded to work her way through college while employed at night at a Miami hotel as a switchboard operator and living as a housekeeper in a motel. On graduation she became manager of a large group of villas.

Continuing educational opportunities such as these are to be found throughout the country. The movement began only about a decade ago, with Radcliffe College, the Universities of Minnesota and Wisconsin, and Carnegie Tech in the forefront. Now more than two thousand schools in fifty states teach more than fifty thousand courses for adults. Many church organizations offer courses, and so do Ys, Jewish community centers, and county agricultural agencies. The Veterans Administration makes it possible for adults to avail themselves of many opportunities.

One of those who did so was Mrs. Sybil Kelly, a New York mother who worked for years as a seamstress to help support her four children because her husband's wages were insufficient. She managed to keep on working and at the same time to enroll in the City University's Discovery Program for the disadvantaged. While she was earning her bachelor's and master's degrees in social work, her children attended schools on full scholarships they earned on their own merits.

The Institute of Awareness in Philadelphia was established to provide education for women, beginning with afternoon classes to fit the leisure-time schedules of most housewives. Mary Gaynor, chairman of the institute, reported that women from twenty-five to sixty-eight appeared for the initial sessions, some of them quite frankly seeking ways to overcome their guilt over staying at home and others hoping to become paraprofessionals in the fields of mental health or library work or teaching. One woman went to college to learn how to handle the property of her husband, who had been hospitalized for three years. Another with a college degree found that a job was not her answer. She attended the course at the urging of her two college-age children, who wanted her to do something with her education. "I felt so terrible," she said. "I didn't enjoy my home. I felt I should be doing *something.* I didn't even know what I wanted to do." But after she had finished a course on developing her potential, she decided that all she really wanted to do was to stay at home and enjoy it; the course had helped her get rid of her guilt.

Syracuse University began its "While You Were Away" Program of continuing education for women in 1963, within the Humanistic Study Center and Center for Continuing Education for Women. Although designed for middle-aged women, as was the case in Philadelphia, younger ones also enrolled in courses in fine arts, economics, child development, library sciences, forestry, music, theater, political science, geography, and anthropology.

"There's always room for trained maturity," said Mary Gilmore Smith, counselor at the Syracuse center. She finds that women appear to be frightened when they first return to the academic world, but they soon get over their timidity. One middle-aged student had been reared by a father who did not believe in education for girls; now that her children were grown, she decided to get the schooling she had always wanted. On receiving her degree she became a teacher in her home community. That experience led Mrs. Smith to conclude: "I would encourage any woman to think in terms of herself as a whole individual, as a contributing person as well as a receiving one in our society, and not to hesitate to turn to the source of assistance that will make her more able to express herself fully, no matter what her age is."

"Repentant dropouts" is the way Katharine Byrne, director of Mundelein College's degree-completion program, views the three hundred mature Chicago women who have studied at her school. She said that more than 500,000 "quiet revolutionaries"—mature women—had infiltrated the college campuses while their children were rioting for their "rights." More than half the women had started college as teenagers but dropped out. Most were housewives with children in their teens or beyond who found after years of "amiable amateurism" that their services were important enough to merit remuneration. Mrs. Byrne recalled one who had worked as a volunteer in a mental-health clinic and who had returned to school to study psychology so she could do something other than file case histories. Another sought a degree in religious education. The mother of a handicapped child wanted to learn to help him.

"Why do I want a degree?" one of the women asked. "Because I am the only person I know who is over twenty-two and doesn't have one—or more. It's humiliating."

Another wanted to be able to contribute more than Christmas baskets to Spanish-speaking migrants. A woman who had been a precinct captain for years sought a degree in urban sociology. As Mrs. Byrne noted, "Their goals are modest; they do not wish to destroy the campus; they just want to find a parking space within a mile of it."

In 1970 Mrs. Lillian Gardner was one of fifty-three women in the first graduating class of the University of

Rhode Island's continuing-education program for women. At the age of forty-seven, before an audience that included her husband, six children—among them a son who was in her class—and a granddaughter, Mrs. Gardner graduated as a member of two honor societies and went on to teach English. During her college career she managed to keep house, doing her homework between chores. "I'd get up early and throw the wash into the machine," she related. "When I came back, I threw it in the dryer. I ran to the store sometimes in between. I did the ironing when I had a minute. My books were propped on top of the oven while my baking was inside. It's just organization."

CHAPTER 8

Retirement: Time to Take a New Lease on Life

MARY BROWN IS in her early fifties. Her husband, at sixty-two, is planning an early retirement this year. This has put Mary, a successful radio producer, into a quandary: Should she retire too, at the peak of her success in a well-paying career she enjoys, and then share fully in her husband's plan for putting sunrise into his sunset years?

Actually the question is far more complicated than that, for she must think about what will happen to her marriage if she continues to work while her husband is tapering off and finding new interests. What will their income be if they both retire? Where will they live? What will happen to their standard of living? Can she and her husband find creative activities in common that will bring them closer together, make their last years more fruitful and, at the same time, provide her with creative outlets that will compensate for her leaving a position it has taken her years to achieve?

Her situation is quite different from that of Jane Smith,

who has managed to reap her own kind of rewards by being active without holding a job. Jane has been a devoted wife, mother, housewife, and true helpmeet to her husband. She has busied herself with the PTA, the garden club, and occasional bridge games with old friends. Although her children have gone off to lives of their own, she has stuck to a well-organized schedule that has kept her days filled. Now her husband is talking about giving up his important job in an advertising agency and becoming a full-time writer. They are financially secure, but Jane is upset about his desire to change careers in middle age. Their marriage is a good one—they get along well—but she is concerned about what will happen if he stays at home all day "getting underfoot" and possibly upsetting her carefully planned schedule.

"I heard a joke," she said, "about a woman who declared that she married her husband for better or for worse—but *not* for lunch! Now I'm going to be that woman, and I'm afraid I don't think it is very funny."

Elizabeth Gray's circumstances present still another set of problems. She is a working widow whose children are grown but who must support herself until she reaches sixty-five, the mandatory retirement age in the company where she has been a secretary since the death of her husband ten years ago. Now in her mid-fifties, Elizabeth still has plenty of time to plan ahead, which she must do, because her income from Social Security and a small pension will not be enough, particularly if inflation continues. She is also concerned about how she will use her time when she no longer has to go to a nine-to-five job. She hopes to travel, but doubts that she would enjoy doing so alone. So her principal question is: How can she take the fullest advantage of her remaining working years to build additional income to provide security, to develop friends with whom she can do things, and to outline a future for herself that will be both comfortable and enjoyable and prevent her from becoming a burden to her children?

Then there is the woman who has never married; Florence Bucknell is one of those. She has worked most of her life and is an executive secretary making $15,000 a year, with both a generous pension and Social Security in sight. Through the years, she has built a savings account earmarked for medical emergencies in her old age. She has invested wisely, a little at a time, owns a small cottage in Arizona where she plans to move when she retires, and is planning to devote as much time as possible to her lifelong desire to be an artist. While financially secure, she has her problems, the principal one being loneliness. Because she has no relatives, she faces the challenge of finding ways to meet people and build a social life when she moves to Arizona. She also needs some meaningful activities to fill part of her time.

These are examples of the problems that can confront any of us as we move toward what sometimes are billed as the golden years. Whether married or single, a woman is well advised to look as far ahead as possible and to start planning as early as she can. Retirement can be the richest period of life—or the poorest. The secret lies in thinking about it positively long before the time comes to apply for Social Security and Medicare rather than avoiding it with dread. Unfortunately, young people of the now generation—they want everything now, not tomorrow or the next day—tend to shy from the mere thought of old age. We do not feel that one must forgo the pleasures of young life in the hope of a rosy tomorrow, but we do believe that more can and should be done to encourage those in their twenties and thirties to start thinking about their future security instead of leaving it to someone else.

This is particularly necessary because of the increasing numbers opting for early retirement. Some are leaving long-held jobs to fulfill cherished ambitions to pursue other careers, often in fields new to them. Management experts are encouraging companies to allow executives to retire in their late forties and their fifties with realistic pensions, so they can go into public service, teaching, or other fields in which they could share the fruits of their maturity, knowledge, and experience. All of society would gain from this—the worker himself, the organizations he would be able to serve, and the younger men in business who could then move up faster to positions of responsibility.

Such "occupational renewal" is supported by E. Raymond Corey, head of the executive education faculty at the Harvard University Graduate School of Business. He favors a program whereby companies would offer retirement at half pay after twenty years' employment. Included would be required courses of training for a second career in which a retired person could make major contributions by working in government, education, or nonprofit institutions such as hospitals, churches, and charitable organizations that are unable to meet the pay scale of business and industry but need the same kind of expertise.

That is all very well for the corporate executive, who at half pay would still be doing all right. However, most of us cannot afford early retirement—or even retirement at sixty-five—and know that we will have to pinch pennies to make ends meet and use ingenuity in planning activities that will not be a drain on the exchequer. Max Wylie, the television and magazine writer and brother of the late Philip Wylie, who knocked Mom off her pedestal in his 1940s book *A Generation of Vipers,* is able to pass along some good advice as a result of his service as public-relations director of a large Connecticut community in which a third of the people are retired. He has noted how some have managed the "crisis of retirement"; but he also expresses surprise at how poorly prepared most men and women are for the day they collect their last paychecks. Writing in *Family Health,* he urged people regardless of age to think ahead and act in advance to escape some of the pitfalls of retirement.

"What is so hard about retiring?" asks Mr. Wylie. "For one thing, it overtakes most people too quickly. Not too soon, just too *fast.* Retirement comes so abruptly that the peace or exhilaration they had dreamed of proves an illusion. At the beginning, especially, they feel they are marking time mindlessly, waiting for things to happen that do not happen. Their minds fill with fear and loss and with a confusion that, if not cleared up quickly, can soon deepen into almost suicidal depression."

Mr. Wylie also pointed out that retirement sometimes is much harder on a wife; if her husband is unhappy, she may experience a keen sense of *personal* failure. In an effort to guide a woman in such a situation, he suggested that she begin by taking a good look at herself well in advance of her husband's retirement and seek ways to make herself more attractive, setting an example for her husband and encouraging him to spruce up a bit himself. Mr. Wylie also suggests that both husband and wife need to seek pursuits of their own so they do not have too much togetherness and risk getting on each other's nerves. At the same time he feels that it is a good idea to keep the same regular hours and engage in a variety of projects on a schedule that they try to stick to. Further, he urges that a couple give thought in advance to where they want to live in retirement, basing their decisions on their health, income, and interests.

Other ideas he advanced included developing a habit of doing things for others as a way of retarding the aging process and volunteering a regular portion of time to a specific cause or institution. "The people around me who seem happiest in retirement," Mr. Wylie reported, "are those who are most continuously and productively occupied, who have filled part of their own days—and evenings—with activities of their own choosing."

The term *hobby* is often derided, but Mr. Wylie favors avocations as a way to fill time constructively and also as an avenue to new friends with mutual interests. "Even at age fifty, maybe you don't know nearly enough about yourself," he says. "It is not too late to explore; in fact, it's a good time to do it. You've never been so free."

PLANNING AHEAD FOR RETIREMENT

It may not be too late to plan for retirement, but it is never too soon to do so, whether it be building a nest egg or seeking ways to make leisure a full-time "career." No one should wait beyond the age of fifty-five—ten years before retirement—to start doing something about it, in the opinion of the experts we consulted. Just as adolescents plan ahead for their working years, so middle-agers should be giving serious thought to what is going to happen to them after sixty-five. There are several possible ways to begin: First, estimate how much money you will need and where it will come from; think about how you can bulwark yourself against high medical expenses and how you can regulate your basic living costs in the face of inflation. Then put all of your personal affairs in order by deciding where to live and reviewing your will. You will also want to consult your lawyer about other matters and possibly discuss your financial situation with a broker or banker.

Of course, retirement is not that simple. We are trying to present a few guidelines merely as a starting point for individuals such as those we described at the beginning of the chapter and for anyone who has taken the trouble to read this book. Planning can be complicated by early retirement, for example, which enlarges the money problem because Social Security and corporate pensions are lower than they would be at age sixty-five. Personal savings and annuities must be spread over more years, so the income from them is less. Many couples have diversified their assets and should scrutinize closely every possible source of income before deciding that early retirement is for them.

The Institute of Life Insurance has recommended taking the following steps in evaluating your financial situation.

1. What are your resources? List all the financial assets on which you can rely for income after retirement; nothing is too insignificant to include. Social Security and a company pension are obvious sources; there are others that might not come to mind so readily. Be sure to include everything you can think of.

2. What will each resource provide in a lump sum or in regular income? In computing this seek help from experts such as your life-insurance agent or someone at the local Social Security office.

3. How will you use the resources you have? Will you buy a home or rent? Do you need to buy a car? How much can you spend on travel?

In other words, what you are working up to is a budget for retirement, including which assets to use for ongoing expenses, which to set aside for emergencies, and which to keep for the benefit of your family (in other words, your estate).

After estimating what you can reasonably expect as income, you will now need to try to determine how far it will go toward meeting expenses. It is important for a husband and wife to sit down together to work this out, itemizing the fixed expenses they will have in retirement and the expenses they will no longer have, such as transportation to work, lunches, and larger clothing and cleaning bills. Although job-regulated expenses will dry up, there will be higher costs for recreation, and those should be listed, too.

The tax picture usually changes, for the better, upon retirement. Federal income-tax laws provide special savings, such as double exemptions for those over sixty-five.

Social Security payments are tax free, and special federal provisions have been made governing pensions and annuities and income from life insurance. State laws vary widely, however, so it is best to consult your local tax department.

As the Institute of Life Insurance points out, retired persons must be prepared to receive their income on a different basis than they did while working. Instead of the weekly, biweekly, or monthly salary check, income may arrive at various times. Dividends from securities will be in the mail quarterly. Proceeds from the sale of a wheat or corn crop will arrive annually. A corporate pension check may come at a different time of the month than the Social Security payment. The new income pattern may necessitate a new spending program and closer budgeting. As long as you know what will be coming in over any specific period, it is possible to plan ahead.

SOCIAL SECURITY— ONLY PART OF THE ANSWER

Although Social Security is the basic source of retirement income for most people, it provides only subsistence for those who have no other resources. The Social Security program was not created to provide people with all the money they need in their old age; it is a cushion that makes a financially secure retirement possible for those who have been able to make additional provisions. Living at even a moderate level in a large city in 1972 cost a couple about $450 a month, including rent. Social Security payments fall short of this mark, but they are all that many have.

Whether opting for retirement at sixty-two, with smaller Social Security payments, or waiting for the maximum at sixty-five, one should work out the details in advance with the nearest Social Security office. To be assured of receiving your first check soon after retiring, it is necessary to apply at least three months in advance. You should take with you your Social Security card, proof of age, marriage and/or divorce records, and, if you are qualified for survivor benefits, a copy of your spouse's death certificate.

There is no need to go into detail here on the payment schedules, but we would like to comment on one major inequity that penalizes women—the provision that a husband may receive the full maximum monthly payment, while his wife gets somewhat less. In other words, a married woman who has worked all her life and has paid Social Security taxes on exactly the same basis as a man is not entitled under present law to receive as much retirement income as her husband; only the unmarried, the widowed, and the divorced receive the maximum.

The situation has led a number of elderly couples to live in what has been called "sunset sin" in old-age ghettos in Florida, Arizona, and California. They are the widows and widowers who live together for companionship but dare not marry lest the woman's income be reduced. In an effort to correct the inequity, Representative Robert H. Steele of Connecticut introduced a bill that would provide uniform Social Security benefits regardless of sex or marital status. Congressional wags immediately dubbed it the "Steele Senility Sex Bill"!

PENSIONS CAN HELP TOO

Thousands of companies, large and small, have pension plans or profit-sharing programs for their employees as supplements to Social Security, but seldom is the combination sufficient. Moreover, only about a third of those currently covered by such plans will ever receive monthly checks, according to an analysis made by George P. Schultz when he was Secretary of Labor in the Nixon administration. Most workers forfeit their benefits by quitting before they have qualified for pensions. Only a minority have the staying power to remain with one employer throughout their working lives, or even the twenty years usually required for a pension. A wage earner may switch jobs three or four times during his productive years, never remaining long enough to look forward to a pension. Many find themselves without security when they are laid off in slack times. Irwin Ross, writing in *Harvest Years,* a magazine published for the retired, attributes failure to guarantee adequate security to weak provisions for vesting employees' interests in pension plans and generally lax enforcement.

Vesting is a nonforfeitable right to a pension at a set age, which an employee retains when he leaves a job before he is qualified for full retirement benefits. Generally, it is a deferred right, with the worker at age sixty or sixty-five drawing a pension that is usually a partial payment depending on length of service. Mr. Ross suggested several improvements: mandatory vesting after ten years' service, or graduated vesting beginning after six years and increasing by 10 per cent a year thereafter, so that an employee is 50 per cent vested after ten years and fully vested after fifteen.

"Portability," which would allow an employee to transfer pension credits from one company to another, has also been suggested, along with improved funding standards that would protect employer and employee alike. Senator Jacob K. Javits of New York was the author of a bill that would include both the graduated vesting principle and funding procedures that would guarantee solvency. He also proposed a federal insurance program for pension plans; a central fund to serve as a pension clearinghouse; rules governing conflict of interest, graft, and wrongdoing; and creation of a new federal commission on pensions and employee benefits.

Employees should read pension plans carefully to make sure of their provisions. It is advisable to check periodically with the personnel office about your status in the pension plan rather than waiting until you are on the brink of retirement, when it is too late to correct errors. If, on leaving a company, you have a vested interest, get a written statement spelling out your rights and keep the pension office informed of your whereabouts until it is time to start receiving your checks.

BUILDING AN ESTATE IS AN ART

Some people manage to practice thrift all their lives, even on modest incomes, building savings accounts or equity in homes or other property or amassing tidy holdings in stocks and bonds that assure them a measure of financial security in their later years. Not all of us are lucky enough, provident enough, or wise enough to be able to do that, but there are other potential sources of income that can keep us out of the poorhouse. To supplement Social Security and pensions, we may be able to fall back on the cash value of a life-insurance policy or an annuity. A person can begin paying into an annuity only a few years before retirement; the payments are larger than they would have been had he started at an earlier age, but the benefits can be significant.

The need for protection that causes men—and sometimes women—to buy insurance to guarantee a college education for children or to backstop a mortgage decreases with age. Most people start pruning their insurance coverage after their children are grown, but protection is often needed in retirement, particularly for widows, when two Social Security checks are no longer coming in.

An insurance policy can be terminated on retirement and the cash value paid to the holder. He may also opt for continued payment of premiums to protect his heirs or he may convert a life policy to another type of coverage or an annuity. Financial advisers say that while taking the money in a lump sum may be a momentary boon, it also may become difficult, expensive, or even impossible to take out insurance again if it is needed. Paying premiums is costly for those who need every penny they have just to exist. Conversion can bring a fixed income, but offers no protection against inflation; it also permanently ties up capital. Life insurance pays if you die, while an annuity pays if you live. A single woman needs a larger income in addition to a pension and Social Security payments than does a couple. Although her cost of living might be only 75 per cent of that of a couple, she will have to find additional income to make up for the fact that she is getting only one Social Security check. Even a $10,000 annuity policy would pay only about $75 a month, so she would be wise to have additional savings, and she might consider increasing her annuity.

There is a wide variety of annuities and methods of paying for them. Some provide little if anything for heirs and have no cash or loan value for an emergency; others contain life-insurance clauses and can be borrowed on at low rates of interest. In planning as practically and as far in advance as possible, you should check with your insurance agent or banker, who is there to help you, and shop around before you buy either a policy or an annuity or convert the policy you have. Also investigate alternative investment opportunities and try not to put all of your nest egg into one basket. At the same time, you should have a cash reserve for emergencies. Knowing where your next nickel is coming from may help you live longer;

it certainly will enable you to get more enjoyment out of your retirement.

WHERE SHALL I RETIRE TO?

Choosing a retirement haven is one of the most important aspects of later life. Where can I enjoy the best possible health with the least financial and emotional strain? Where is life the easiest? Should I sell my home and buy or rent a smaller one? Would it be best to move to a warmer climate, or would I be happier to stay where I have lived so many years? Do I want to be near my children or other relatives or old friends? Would it be best to live near educational, cultural, and recreational facilities so that I will be assured of plenty of things to do? Should I pull up stakes for a while and travel, and set new roots later?

Finances probably will unlock the answers to those questions for you. Housing costs are the chief concern of retired people living on fixed incomes. Those who have paid off their mortgages and plan to stay put are fortunate, but widows and older unmarried women may not have such good luck. Many people with no other place to go settle down happily in retirement communities or senior citizens' homes, while others balk at the notion of being isolated from different age groups.

The state of one's health and the style of life sought are also determining factors in selecting a locale. Those who can afford it may seek the most ideal year-round climate, using preretirement vacations to shop for the right place, possibly one in which they already have friends. It is becoming more likely that older people who have occupied the same home for a number of years will, on retirement, find themselves stuck in deteriorating neighborhoods or confronted with prohibitive taxes. They are forced to move against their will and find apartments or buy cooperatives or condominiums, which offer some tax advantages and relieve them of maintenance chores and the unforeseen expenses that confront homeowners with nagging regularity. Mobile homes have become popular among retired persons, but before committing yourself, you should be aware that "mobile" is a misnomer unless you plan to haul a relatively small trailer behind your car. The standard mobile home is mobile in that it is towed to a lot in a mobile-home community; there it is mounted on a small foundation and linked to the water, sewer, gas, and electrical systems. The "mobile" home is now rooted among a dense cluster of similar prefabricated structures, with the neighbors next door only a whisper away.

For those who can afford it, a commercial "retirement village" development may be the answer; but one should be prepared for the fact that the community will be composed entirely of older people. Also, one should be forewarned that some of the highly promoted settlements do not always live up to their billing. The necessity of visiting the community and asking every kind of question about the housing, facilities, costs, etc., cannot be overemphasized. There have been cases of retired people who have plunged their life savings into a mirage. Therefore, do not be pressured by free dinner parties hundreds or thousands of miles from the site of a prospective home. If you accept an invitation to make an "inspection tour," insist on getting off the beaten path so that you can look at more than the model home on display and so that you can see all of the recreational facilities, shopping centers, and other fringe conveniences. It is a good idea to find out about transportation services to the nearest town to make sure that you are not buying your way into an old-age "prison."

In writing *The New Years and New Middle Age,* Anne Simon became convinced that the American concept of retirement is "the greatest hoax we've played on ourselves as a society." She abhors retirement villages as urban creations that isolate the aged from the rest of society. "I really cannot imagine," she says, "why we swallowed this thing so passively and so willingly except that we are so terrified of being older that, in a way, we let anything be done to us as a punishment rather than stand up and say, 'Why am I no longer a functioning being?' "

Those who want to be closer to the center of things can choose among retirement homes, apartments, and hotels that offer individual privacy along with communal facilities such as dining rooms, medical-care centers, reading rooms, lounges, and game rooms. These are particularly comforting places for the person alone, for there is always someone handy in emergencies or moments of loneliness. Places of this sort are often operated on a nonprofit basis by unions, churches, and other organizations. Federally sponsored public-housing projects for older people are also available in a number of areas, as are local housing accommodations with rent supplements provided by municipalities for those with low incomes.

It is estimated that 14 per cent of older people live with their children or other relatives, but such togetherness is not encouraged by many sociologists and psychologists. Only recently we heard an older person say, "I love my daughter dearly, but I could have learned to hate her easily if I had continued living with her." Familiarity in such a case can and does breed contempt. It is much better when one can say, "I have my own tiny apartment and we are the best of friends."

WHAT IS LEISURE?

With the advent of the three-day holiday weekends scattered through the year, shorter workdays and longer vacations, and the prospect of a four-day work week, questions about leisure cannot wait until retirement to be answered. Most of us are already finding more free time for personal pursuits than we had when we were younger, and far more than our parents and grandparents had. Learning to use this free time to the fullest in our middle years will help us avoid the frustrations of idleness in later life.

More and more economists, labor leaders, and workers favor a four-day week, partly as a means of alleviating such urban problems as traffic jams, overloaded public transit systems, pollution, and overtaxed restaurants and recreational facilities. At least sixty major businesses already have adopted the four-day week. It sounds unrealistic and downright uneconomical to opponents; the arguments are much the same as they were when Saturdays off were proposed only a few decades ago.

Because total working hours are decreasing, perhaps we can look forward eventually to three days of work and four of leisure. Riva Poor, editor of *4 days, 40 hours,* holds the view that husbands on a four-day week may tend to take a larger role in family life, helping with household chores and shopping. Others, of course, would use their time off to train for or enter a second career, just as many people are "moonlighting" today. With much of the drudgery now removed from housework, wives should be able to find time to share their husbands' added time off. As far as Mrs. Poor is concerned, leisure should not present any problems; "it's a benefit," she declared.

That is more or less the term the Greeks had for it. They believed that work existed to provide leisure, without which there could be no culture. If this is true, our added leisure should make our entire society far more cultured than it is. The quality of leisure is all important; concern about how it is used is expressed increasingly by behavioral scientists and psychologists. That was the main concern of a 1969 conference on "Educating for the New Leisure" at the University of California at Riverside, where educators were urged to regard recreation as *re*-creation, for people need to utilize fully their physical, mental, and social capacities at play as well as at work.

"Eventually all people must accept the responsibility for themselves in relation to their free time and the full development of their lives," declared William H. Ridinger, chairman of recreation and outdoor entertainment at Southern Illinois University. "As dedicated professionals, most of us feel responsible for our fellow men and want to help them in one way or another to make 'time live' rather than 'kill time'; to enrich themselves rather than enslave themselves; and to become self-realized and fulfilled rather than self-defeated and empty of joy and happiness."

Expanding on that view, Lawrence Suhm, director of the Leisure Research and Development Institute of Madison, Wisconsin, said: "We are free when our lives are uncommitted, but not free to be what we were intended to be. Real freedom is not freedom *from* but freedom *for*. This is what I think leisure is all about—it is a kind of freedom to be or to do what we are intended to become or do as human beings. In this more positive sense, leisure is the freedom we attain which can be made use of for the development and utilization of our human capacities."

It was this freedom that Lucile Rood, a former journalist, was seeking when she started working on *How to Find Leisure Time and Use It Creatively* as a guide for the busy woman. "No one seemed to have any leisure to use," she found. "All of their time seemed to be devoted to making a *living*, leaving no time for making a *life.*" Mrs. Rood, who died recently, lived well into her eighties, enjoying a vital and exciting retirement. She recognized that one solution to better living lies in more constructive use of leisure for the enrichment of lives "that are feeding on the monotony of greater efficiency, more money, bigger houses, faster automobiles, and are starving for the enjoyment that comes from leisurely living, social intercourse, deeper and faster friendships based on cultural development."

MAKING THE MOST OF YOUR TIME WHEN TIME IS ALL YOU HAVE

In some ways learning to use leisure creatively is more important for women than for men. Why? It enables wives to enjoy with their husbands the kind of companionship that can flow into retirement. The mother who knows what to do when "there is nothing to do" can help her children learn to spend rather than waste otherwise empty hours. Because most women outlive their husbands, learning to use leisure can help them over some rough spots in their widowhood. To spare herself from the loneliness of life without a man, a woman should start by building a circle of friends who really mean something to her. Jean Kinney, the writer, points out that the only way a woman is going to meet "interesting people is to become interesting people." Then she is ready to reach out to another person with similar interests; if neither is feigning enthusiasm, a meaningful relationship may blossom.

For the woman who has always been alone, retirement poses special problems. In a study entitled *The Psychological Aspects of Retirement,* Harold Geist, a consulting psychologist, has observed that the single woman tends to withdraw increasingly into herself during her later working years. This, he says, is just the opposite of what she should do. Because she lacks the norms of family life and family groups, he explains, she should reach out in her last working years to try to find other groups to make up for the absence of a family. This becomes all the more necessary for the single woman because she is likely to be less financially secure than the married woman in retirement.

Dr. Geist also noted that a professional woman who has struggled for years to make it in a man's world feels a sudden loss of prestige on retiring; she has identified so closely with her job that it has become her identity. Her sense of loss requires special compensatory activity through which she can gain new recognition and a new identity. While he feels strongly about this, Dr. Geist acknowledged that retirement to some professional women means a much-needed and longed-for relief from a daily schedule; it gives them time to rest and a chance to do things with no special challenges, just for fun. Diversified interests beyond those of their careers tend to ease the adjustment to retired status.

Married women are more likely to retire—and retire early—than single women, who frequently hang on as long as they can. There are two basic reasons for this: The unmarried woman may need to earn an income as long as she is able to work, and she may need to have something that she *must* do every day. About half of all working women, most of them married, are glad to turn in their desk keys at sixty or sixty-five because they prefer leisure or volunteer activities and also possibly because they regard their role as wage-earner to be secondary to the roles of wife and homemaker. Of course, it can be argued that a housewife never retires, although her life may change when her husband stops working.

Opportunities abound for recreation and social life, for travel, for education, and for development of new skills and hobbies. For those who want to express themselves or broaden their outlooks, libraries have shelves of "how-to" guides to hobbies; and most high schools, community centers, Ys, and park recreation departments offer classes that cost little or nothing. There are many do-it-yourself courses in which one may learn plumbing, furniture repair, and the fundamentals of construction, as well as other skills. Auto mechanics' courses enable you to know your car. For those with a little cash to play around with, there are courses in investing. As a fringe benefit, all such courses give the participants a chance to get to know one another and lay the groundwork for new friendships.

Cultural pursuits are available to residents of larger cities, and not all of them require a cash outlay. A study of local newspapers will uncover free lectures, concerts, book discussions, and other intellectual fare for which no admission is charged. The person with a budget allowing for the purchase of tickets has far more opportunities, of course. Even small towns are visited by touring lecturers, concert artists, orchestras, ballet and theatrical companies, and other groups. Some find that only in their retirement are they able to take advantage of what is available in their cities—zoos, museums, galleries, planetariums, aquariums, botanical gardens, and similar attractions. Walking tours are offered in a number of places, as are archaeological field trips and science workshops. If you really look for something to do, you can find it.

One of the ironies of life is that most of us work hard all our lives, dreaming of travels we would like to take when we retire, only to find that when we reach the point where we have the time, we lack the money. The picture has been brightened somewhat by the introduction of reduced off-season rates for senior groups. Sometimes organized tours begin long before the party leaves home, with discussion groups and even seminars on the languages of the places to be visited. The retired person has time to learn about the areas he plans to tour; study of the customs, art, and food enriches a visit to a strange place.

For the stay-at-homes there can be no more rewarding retirement activity than serving others. Fred Faassen, president of the American Association of Retired Persons, maintains that "unless we are involved in helping someone else, we are not going to find satisfaction either during our first career in the business and professional world or in our second career of retirement." He cites several factors that lead to a happy retirement; the first among them is self-respect, which comes from having a purpose in life through contributing to a better society. Also important to Faassen are maintaining contact with people, which provides much of the same satisfaction that was derived from associating with colleagues during the working years, and doing something that gains recognition and respect from others.

THE VALUE OF VOLUNTEER WORK

Few things we can do are as rewarding as helping others. Service organizations struggling against ever-tighter budgets rely more and more on volunteers; there are plenty of jobs to be done in any community. While having a skill helps, most of the talents needed are ones that most people have—reading, talking, typing, cooking, knowing how to work with children, or being interested in current affairs. The secret of being a successful volunteer is to do your best at whatever job you are assigned. Every woman has some talent. As Jean Kinney said, "I don't like to drive a car, so I should never volunteer to take people to the polls or become a driver for someone because it is a concern to me. But I happen to like to write, so I believe that I should volunteer my services only as a writer." She suggests that the potential volunteer list her likes and dislikes and then try to use five of the things she likes in some way every day, either as a volunteer, at home, or on the job.

There is something for everyone in volunteer work. If you like children, you can become a volunteer storyteller or offer to play games with children, plan trips for them, or serve lunches at day-care or neighborhood centers, playgrounds, or schools. If your concern lies mainly with the very old, there are nursing homes, senior-citizen centers, and even individual residences occupied by the lonely and infirm where you can read, write letters, or fill a void just by chatting. Youth groups and community centers can always use another leader or someone to teach special skills. The lonely, the sick, and the handicapped, whether in hospitals, foreign-student centers, clinics, health agencies, or Red Cross groups, need help or companionship. Poverty programs, race-relations organizations, political parties, and community cultural groups also need volunteers.

A volunteer effort that has been mushrooming across the country is service at telephone centers where people call with problems. The largest of the scores of services of this type is the Help Line Telephone Center at Marble Collegiate Church in New York, which operates around the clock, every day of the year, with two hundred trained volunteers backed up by a staff of professionals to deal with everything from leaky plumbing to mental breakdown. Hundreds of calls are made to Help Line every month by people—most of them elderly—who are simply lonely. A large number of the volunteers serving Help Line and the many other similar centers are retired people who give a few hours or a day or two every week. Many of the independent telephone centers are sponsored by community groups, and nearly two score are church-sponsored and affiliated through a national accrediting organization. It may be possible for a retired person to get such a center started at his church if he can win the support of the rest of the congregation.

A careful reading of your daily newspaper or a visit to City Hall, the local chamber of commerce, or a service club may uncover ways in which you can be of service. New York City, for example, has a recruitment clearinghouse with the slogan "Have a Heart, Lend a Hand" that has attracted thousands of volunteers. Any community health and welfare council should also be able to direct you to groups in need of volunteers. So too can the National Center for Voluntary Action, with headquarters at 1735 I Street N.W., Washington, D.C. 20006, which encourages education and training in volunteer administrative work and coordinates and encourages local efforts.

Being a volunteer has been the career of Mrs. Marian Mulryan, a Los Angeles grandmother who serves a variety of causes. Her assignments include the regional chairmanship of volunteers for the American Red Cross in the West, in which capacity she counsels and supervises thirteen chapters. She has been associated for more than fifteen years with the Red Cross Basic Management School at Charlottesville, Virginia, and has been a key planner for the California Association of Health and Welfare. One of her greatest achievements was leading thirty-five thousand volunteers, most of them women, in a successful United Crusade.

Mrs. Mulryan believes that a volunteer should bring to her work the same dedication she would have if she were receiving a salary. It is important, she declares, for a volunteer to give generously of her talents and time and be imaginative in what she does. She also should be ready and willing to assume leadership when asked to do so.

A movement to upgrade the status of volunteers is being spearheaded by Ellen Sulzberger Straus, who a few years ago founded "Call for Action" for WMCA, New York, her husband's radio station. The program helped 150,000 New Yorkers with problems ranging from drug addiction to television repairs. Volunteers are the mainstay. Supported by the National Urban Coalition, the program has spread to twenty-four independent radio stations across the country, with more than two thousand women serving as volunteers.

For her persistence in promoting the program, Mrs.

Straus received the 1970 Woman of Conscience Award from the National Council of Women. At that time she proposed that a new job category be established: the professional volunteer. This she defines as "one who would be hired, fired, trained, instructed, appreciated, supervised—indeed, *everything except paid.*" The professional volunteer would undertake a continuing job, whether for one day or five days a week, over an extended period; her hours would be set by the organization she was asked to serve as well as by any union with paid employees on the staff. She would be asked to assure her supervisors that she would be on the job as regularly as if she were being paid. In exchange, the professional volunteer could expect good working conditions, out-of-pocket expenses required to perform her work, and the right to deduct from her income taxes an amount corresponding to the minimum hourly wage for the total hours she contributed. (At present the hours contributed to a worthy cause, regardless of expertise involved, count for nothing on your tax return.) Addressing herself to this situation, Mrs. Straus declared, "If a gift of money is deductible, surely a gift of one's time and talent should be also."

To encourage women to continue serving as dedicated volunteers, Mrs. Straus urges that they be allowed to write "professional volunteer" instead of "housewife" on forms requesting their occupations.

One to whom Mrs. Straus addressed her remarks was Kitty Carlisle, singing star of the stage and screen and widow of the playwright Moss Hart. Miss Carlisle, the mother of two, was appointed a special consultant to Governor Nelson A. Rockefeller's New York State Women's Program. In discussing her ideas with an audience of fellow volunteers, she related that she became involved in public service only late in life. "When I grew up a couple of generations ago—yes, that's not a slip of the tongue—it was easier to isolate yourself from the problems of society," she declared, "to live in a world of bridge-playing and country-club life. But you know, as one grows older, and my old age will be here around next Tuesday, the best thing that can happen to anyone is to be able to give back some of the good things that you have had in life. I've been very lucky. An awful lot of good things have happened to me, and I think the only thing that makes your growing older years worthwhile is to be able to give them back."

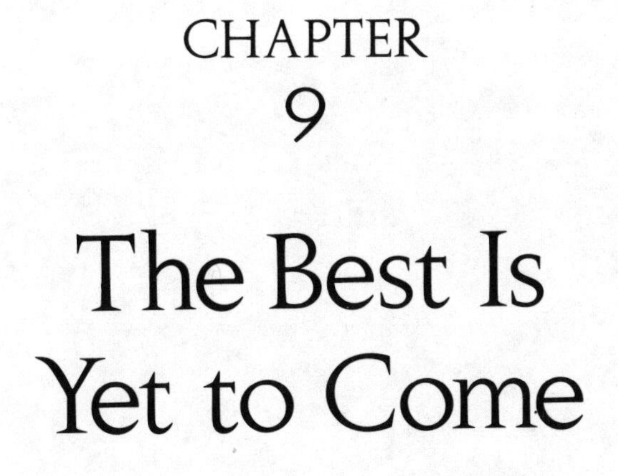

CHAPTER 9

The Best Is Yet to Come

IN THE OPENING pages of this book, we told about several women with problems—problems associated with their middle age. One was a forty-year-old beset by many unexpected pressures: Her mother was ill, her son was threatened with the draft, her husband needed a job, and she was encountering difficulties in completing a term paper in her continuing-education project.

A second woman had awakened to the fact that she was beginning to look "old and fat," and another was an "empty nester" with nothing but time on her hands.

On completing our research on life in the second forties, we decided to check up on these three and find out how they were getting along. We are happy to report that they had found answers to at least some of their problems and that others had solved themselves.

Our first friend reported that her mother was feeling better and was living contentedly in a community for retired people. A mild case of asthma brought a deferment for her son. Her husband had found a good job. And she not only had completed her term paper but had received an A for her effort and was working for an advanced degree in graduate school.

The woman who found herself becoming fat had taken herself in hand; she dieted, joined a gym class, tinted her hair, bought some chic clothes, and emerged looking both slim and stunning. And how she *felt* was more important! She said she never could remember a time when she was more full of pep.

The "empty nester" found a part-time job selling dresses in a department store and was giving of herself as a volunteer reader for the blind. She was tingling with excitement when she told us that "there just aren't enough hours in the day for me to accomplish everything I want to do."

These were now apparently happy and actively contributing women who had stopped feeling sorry for themselves. Does it sound too pat? Too easy? Fiction? Not at all! It simply proves that panic can be a middle-aged woman's worst enemy. Just as she prepares herself to meet the changes of moving from high school to college or to the business world, from college or a job to becoming a wife, a mother, or a careerist, so she must accept the adjustments that are needed in the second half of her life. This period can be the spice of her life if she meets it with the right spirit.

While writing this book, the authors and their husbands found that they had to make radical changes in their own life-styles: One couple moved from a city apartment to a country home; the other went from a very large rented apartment to a small cooperative.

The first couple had divided their time between their apartment, which doubled as the wife's business office during the week, and their home on weekends, holidays, and vacations. An emergency arose requiring that they vacate the apartment. Because the husband had wanted for some time to move permanently to the country and become a willing commuter, the wife responded to the crisis by declaring: "All right. Let's do it. I'll move my office to the country, spend a day or two in town each week, and we can see how it works out. If it doesn't, we can always move back." So off they went, leaving behind the problems and advantages of city living; months later, they were still delighted with the arrangement.

The other pair had lived for more than twenty years in a roomy apartment where they had reared two children and provided a haven for out-of-town guests as well as countless young friends of their children. With the daughter married and the son working abroad, the place had become an empty barn in which the couple rattled around with a nagging feeling that something was always missing. And it was. The laughter and music of the young were gone, except on the occasions of rare visits. The excitement of a family meal had diminished, with only husband and wife sitting down together instead of a group. The size of the apartment had become oppressive, and it far exceeded present needs; but because it was filled with happy memories and mementos, they hung on, frequently talking about the need to make a move and consolidate their possessions to a manageable size, but never having the gumption to do anything about it. There were constant excuses that kept them from making a change—the housing shortage, high rentals, and their own low rent, which made them feel that it would "be a shame to give up a bargain like this."

But then one day they faced their situation squarely; they overcame their lethargy and bought the small cooperative apartment. Then came the painful packing, the terrible decisions about what to do with the surplus furnishings. Shall we take this, sell that, give that away? Must we keep this table, refinish that, junk this, replace that? What about all the books and records? On and on it went, causing mounting anxiety with every day. Finally, the wife paused in the midst of the frenetic activity, looked at her husband, and asked: "Why are we so mournful about leaving this place? This change means *progress.* We'll adjust to the smaller surroundings, be more cheerful with new possessions and a pleasanter neighborhood; and isn't it wonderful that at our ages we feel young enough to plan our future together, to look forward to the years ahead?" That made both of them feel a lot better; they hope it is a harbinger of happier days.

PERIODS OF ADJUSTMENT

Ruth Stafford Peale, wife of Dr. Norman Vincent Peale, the famous minister who has made "positive thinking" a household expression, is a good example of what we have been talking about throughout this book. A positive thinker when it comes to facing the adjustments necessary at each phase of life, Mrs. Peale finds that it is never too late to change and that all of us are going to have to make adjustments as long as we live. As an adult, the first important period of change begins with marriage. "There is always that area of adjustment where a husband and wife can grow together and have the most marvelous time imaginable," she says. The next period of adjustment comes when a mother must learn to relate to growing and developing children. But the most crucial period comes "when her children grow up, go away to school and get married, and she has to let them go," according to Mrs. Peale. "She must fill her life always with enough outside things so that it can continue to be full and rewarding."

At this point, with the children gone, Mrs. Peale points out, a wife has arrived "back at the beginning," alone with her husband, and "if she is mature enough and has enough outside interests, her life will continue to be rewarding. I would say that a woman must prepare all of her life for that period when she lets her children go. Sometimes the greatest and hardest thing for a mother to do is to let her children go, but it's most important in the maturing process of her youngsters."

Mrs. Peale has written a book called *The Adventure of Being a Wife*, reflecting her optimism and her love of life —a useful life. It provides a contrast to the gloominess of many mature women who cannot adjust to change and react instead by burying themselves in unrewarding, unstimulating, unchallenging existences. Mrs. Peale told us that she believes that "being a wife is the greatest career a woman can have. And yet, after she gives her time to being a mother, she still has plenty of time to go out and have a career of her own. I will admit that this requires a great deal of organization on her part. She must plan her day, she must plan her work, she must plan her emphasis. In a way it's an attitude I'm speaking of. I think she has a perfect right to go out in the world and fulfill herself, but my feeling is that the first emphasis really should be on being a wife."

Mrs. Peale speaks with authority, for in addition to being the wife of a busy minister, which requires that she devote considerable time to his activities in and out of the church, she has built her own career; at the same time she has remained slim and chic through regular exercise, including walking, skiing, and swimming, and has remained young in spirit and outlook. Her days are filled with endless activity. She founded and supervises the work of the Foundation for Christian Living, which regularly distributes Dr. Peale's sermons and other writings as well as material written by others to more than 600,000 people around the world, and she conducts a number of other programs with her husband. She is coeditor of *Guideposts* magazine, an inspirational monthly founded by Dr. Peale. Much of her time is devoted to her service as a member of the boards of the American Bible Society and the American Foundation of Religion and Psychiatry, which provides counseling to the troubled and training in pastoral counseling to ministers. She is a trustee of Hope College, a church-related liberal arts college in Holland, Michigan, and is in constant demand as a speaker.

These are only a few of Mrs. Peale's activities, and she says that other women too can find things to do to make their lives interesting if they go out and look for them. "For me, it's always been best to go to a church or a service organization in the community to find what the opportunities are," she observes. "Anyone who goes out will enrich her own life because her horizons will be broadened, and her life will be better as she helps others to make their lives better. I certainly would advise every woman to find something outside of herself and outside of her home where she can give of herself and make a contribution in the world."

A NEW LOOK AT THE POST-WORLD WAR I GENERATION

The report *Indicators of Trends in the Status of American Women,* prepared for the Russell Sage Foundation in 1971 by Abbott L. Ferriss, has helped us to understand some of the social trends that may affect us as women at the midpoint in our lives. The report emphasizes that not only are there more women than men, but their relative numbers will continue to rise, particularly in the over-forty age bracket. Increases are expected in the relative number of widows over widowers and in the number of single women past middle age. While it may be encouraging to know that we can live longer, who wants to live in a world without men? It behooves those of us who have husbands to help give them longer life.

On the economic front, the Russell Sage *Indicator* reports that the number of female heads of households, now totaling about 5.4 million, has been rising at a rate of about 100,000 a year during the last decade. Many of these are older women in the labor force; an increasing proportion are expected to go to work in the future. In order to be effective on the job, we should not wait until we become "rusty ladies" before preparing for employment. Regardless of our age we owe it to ourselves to continue our education by taking advantage of special courses and training programs and otherwise getting ready to enter the labor market better equipped to cope with youthful competition. Likewise, if we face the prospect of being alone or self-supporting in the second half of our lives, we need to sharpen our understanding of money management and of the everyday legalities of life.

Socially, women's organizational affiliations have been shifting, according to the Russell Sage report. We are shucking off some aspects of the mother-homemaker role in favor of wider interests in the community. The report found that women are less interested in sororities, ethnic groups and organizations in which membership is inherited by one generation from another, federated clubs, and rural-life groups. Participation has been increasing in organizations with religious affiliations however, as it has in social service clubs, public affairs groups, and other bodies with wider horizons. Organizations of women in the professions, education, recreation, and social welfare are also growing.

All of this is evidence that change *is* inevitable and that women must prepare to meet change not only in their personal lives but on the broad social scene as well—and at whatever age they happen to be. As for the over-forty woman facing her biological "change of life," we trust that we have established the fact that it will affect her psychological, marital, and sexual well-being only if she allows it to. As long as medical help is available, she should accept it; age becomes a factor only if she lets it become one.

SOME UNFINISHED BUSINESS

Despite the words of the popular commerical "You've come a long way, baby," women are setting new goals that will carry them much further than any of us can now conceive. We live in an exciting period when the wave of women's liberation is beating down walls of male resistance. We have much to offer and we want a chance to participate fully in life before we go "over the hill." It was a little more than a century ago that several hundred women—and men—first met in upstate New York to chart a program of reform for equal rights for women. Through the years, there were brief skirmishes and some minor victories before women finally won the vote a little more than half a century ago. But it was only in the decade of the 1960s that demands for equal pay and equal opportunity, more child-care centers, liberalized abortion laws, increased educational opportunities, equality in law and politics, and more sharing of household responsibilities reached effective proportions.

While "women's lib" may seem on the surface to be a movement principally for the young, it has a great appeal for mature women, for now that we live longer, we want the freedom to utilize our bonus years to their fullest. We do not want to be "kept in our place" psychologically, physically, economically, or socially. Yes, mature women are "one of our nation's most neglected natural resources" and we must recognize ourselves as such. The upgrading of our place generally will help to improve each woman's future role in society.

AUTUMN IS A GREAT TIME OF LIFE

George Santayana wrote in his *Little Essays* that "to be interested in the changing seasons is, in this middling zone, a happier state of mind than to be hopelessly in love with spring." Every woman hopes to find a way to age gracefully. She may find her answer in a rigid discipline of exercise or diet. She may blossom with the help of cosmetics and the latest fashions. She may have her face lifted. But what she does with her mind, energy, and talents as she meets the changing seasons is what really matters. An improved self-image comes not just from her "mirror, mirror on the wall," but also from the reflection in the eyes of the man she loves, her children, her employer, her co-workers, and her friends. What she *does* is the true definer of what she *is.* To feel well physically, to be well groomed, to have an attractive personality, these are desirable goals. But add to this the ability to *belong,* to participate, to cooperate, and to have purpose, and you have a formula for a happy second forty years.

Popularity polls are sometimes an indicator of values in a society. It is significant that for a number of years the Gallup Poll's lists of the ten women most admired by the American people have usually included women in their second forties. Among them have been such obvious choices as Mrs. Dwight D. Eisenhower, Mrs. Lyndon B. Johnson, and Mrs. Richard M. Nixon, all of whom achieved fame as the "powers behind the presidency." But also included have been such self-made women as Senator Margaret Chase Smith, Pearl Buck, Golda Meir, Indira Gandhi, and Helen Hayes—mature women who have been doers.

All of us can be doers. We are unique in that our life begins anew when our childbearing years end. Our attractiveness need not deteriorate. Nor must our sex drives or abilities wane; they can be even greater than when we were younger. The French may refer to us as "women of a certain age." The *certain* thing is that we *can* turn middle age into the prime time of our lives. Welcome to the second forty! Make the most of it, and it will make the most of you!

ACKNOWLEDGMENTS

WE ARE DEEPLY indebted to the many men and women who shared their professional and life experiences with us in the interviews they granted to the news feature service of the Information Center on the Mature Woman and to its transcribed radio program, which is supported by Ayerst Laboratories, and which provided us with much of the basic material incorporated into this book.

We have a special word of appreciation for the center's professional staff—Lynne Abraham, Ruth Bodansky, Jo Coppola, Lydia Edwards, Marie McCormack, and Gloria Miller—for their skillful research and reporting, and also for Harold Mehling for his valuable editorial advice.

Our thanks go also to Faythe Walsh for the interest and loving care she showered on the manuscript in typing it—in the course of which she caught some of the things we overlooked.

We are grateful, indeed, for the patience and interest

of our literary agent, Robert Lewis, and our editor, William Decker, who must have wondered on occasion if we were going to complete this project in our third forty.

SONDRA GORNEY

CLAIRE COX

FOR FURTHER READING

GENERAL

Born Female, Caroline Bird, with Sara Welles Briller. David McKay, 1968.

Culture and Commitment, Margaret Mead. Natural History Press, doubleday, 1970.

Generation in the Middle, report by Blue Cross Association, Vol. XXIII, No. 1, 551 Fifth Avenue, New York, N.Y. 10017, 1970.

The Mature Woman, Anna K. Daniels, M.D. Prentice-Hall, 1953.

The Middle-Age Crisis, Barbara Fried. Harper & Row, 1967.

The New Years—A New Middle Age, Anne W. Simon. Knopf, 1968.

ON MENOPAUSE AND GENERAL HEALTH

Backache, Stress and Tension, Hans Krause, M.D. Simon & Schuster, 1965.

Cancer Facts for Women, American Cancer Society, 219 East 42nd Street, New York, N.Y. 10017.

"Contact Lenses: A Vital Role in Vision Care," American Optometric Association, 130 West 42nd Street, New York, N.Y. 10036.

A Doctor Discusses Menopause, G. Lombard Kelly, M.D. Budlong Press, 1967.

Health in the Later Years, Robert E. Rothenberg, M.D. New American Library, 1964.

How to Live with Diabetes, Henry Dolger, MD., and Bernard Seeman. W. W. Norton, 1958.

"Mature Vision and Its Care," American Optometric Association, 130 West 42nd Street, New York, N.Y. 10036.

Middle Age and Aging, Bernice L. Neugarten. University of Chicago Press, 1968.

The Second Forty Years, Edward Steiglitz, M.D. Lippincott, 1946.

"What to Do When Hearing Fails," American Medical Association, 535 North Dearborn Street, Chicago, Ill., 60610.

When You Grow Older, George Lawton and Maxwell S. Stewart. Public Affairs Pamphlet 131, Public Affairs Committee, New York, N.Y. 10016.

Woman's Choice, Robert Glass, M.D., and Nathan G. Case, M.D. Basic Books, 1970.

Your Menopause, Ruth Carson. Public Affairs Pamphlet 447, Public Affairs Committee, 381 Park Avenue South, New York, N.Y. 10016, 1970.

ON SEX

The Ageless Woman, Sherwin A. Kaufman, M.D. Prentice-Hall, 1967.
An Analysis of Human Sexual Inadequacy, Jhan and June Robbins. New American Library, 1970.
The Conduct of Sex, Lawrence K. Frank, M.A. William Morrow, 1961.
Everything You Always Wanted to Know About Sex—But Were Afraid to Ask, David Reuben. David McKay, 1970.
Human Sexual Inadequacy, W. H. Masters and Virginia E. Johnson. Little, Brown, 1970.
Human Sexual Response, W. H. Masters, M.D., and Virginia E. Johnson. Little, Brown, 1966.
Love and Will, Rollo May, Ph.D. W. W. Norton, 1969.
The Pill: Facts and Fallacies About Today's Oral Contraceptives, Robert W. Kistner, M.D. Delacorte Press, 1968.
Psychology of Women, Vol. II, Helene Deutsch, M.D. Grune & Stratton, 1945.
Sexual Behavior in the Human Female, A. C. Kinsey, et al. W. B. Saunders, 1953.
"Sexual Life in the Later Years," Sex Information and Education Council of the U.S., 1855 Broadway, New York, N.Y. 10023, 1970.

ON WOMEN ALONE

Divorce and After, edited by Paul Bohannan. Doubleday, 1971.
Facing Life Alone, Marian Champagne. Universal Publishing and Distributing, 1969.

Love the Second Time Around, Dorothy Marie Freda. Aladdin Press.

Merry Widow, Grace Fletcher. William Morrow, 1970.

"When You Lose a Loved One," "Divorce," and "The One-Parent Family," pamphlets published by the Public Affairs Committee, 381 Park Avenue South, New York, N.Y. 10016 (25 cents each).

When You're a Widow, Clarissa Start. Concordia, 1968.

Women Alone, Isabella Taves. Funk & Wagnalls, 1968.

The World of the Formerly Married, Morton Hunt. McGraw-Hill, 1966.

ON FAMILY LIFE

How to Be a Good Mother-in-Law and Grandmother, Edith G. Neisser, Public Affairs Pamphlet 174, Public Affairs Committee, 381 Park Avenue South, New York, N.Y. 10016.

How to Stay Married: A Modern Approach to Sex, Money and Emotions in Marriage, Norman Lobsenz, with Clark W. Blackburn. Cowles, 1968.

The Intimate Enemy, George R. Bach, M.D., and Peter Wyden. Morrow, 1969.

Marriage and Love in the Middle Years, James A. Peterson. Public Affairs Pamphlet 456, Public Affairs Committee, 381 Park Avenue South, New York, N.Y. 10016.

Married Love in the Middle Years, James A. Peterson. Association Press, 1968.

A New Look at In-Laws, Erma Pixley. American Institute of Family Relations, Publication 246.

The Person: His Development Throughout the Life Cycle, Theodore Lidz, M.D. Basic Books, 1968.

Personal Understanding of Marriage, Jean J. Rutherford and Robert N. Rutherford, M.D. Budlong Press, 1967.

What Makes a Marriage Happy?, David R. Mace. Public Affairs Pamplet 290, Public Affairs Committee, 381 Park Avenue South, New York, N.Y. 10016.

ON WOMEN IN PUBLIC LIFE

American Woman: The Changing Image, edited by Beverly Benner Cassara. Beacon Press, 1962.

American Women, Report of the President's Commission on the Status of Women, 1963.

American Women, 1963–1968, Report of the Interdepartmental Committee on the Status of Women.

By the Political Sea, Katie Louchheim. Doubleday, 1970.

Modern American Career Women, Eleanor Clymer and Lillian Erlich. Dodd, Mead, 1965.

The Natural Superiority of Women, Ashley Montagu. Macmillan, 1968.

Unbought and Unbossed, Shirley Chisholm. Houghton Mifflin, 1970.

What's on Woman's Future Agenda?, Helen Colton. Family Forum, 1971.

"Women Today," Today Publications and News Service, National Press Building, Washington, D.C. 20004, 1971.

ON LEGAL AND FINANCIAL MATTERS

"Know Your Rights—What a Working Wife Should Know About Her Legal Rights," Harriet F. Pilpel and Minna Post Peyser. Women's Bureau, U.S. Department of Labor, Washington, D.C., 1965.

Legal Rights of Married Women, Daniel J. De Benedictis. Cornerstone Library, 1969.

The Liberated Woman's Appointment Calendar and Sur-

vival Handbook, Lynn Sherr and Jurate Kazickas. Universe Books, 1971.

Marriage and the Law, Harriet F. Pilpel and Theodora Zavin. Collier Books, 1966.

350 Ways to Make Your Money Grow, Faye Henle. Awards Books, 1969.

What Is Happening to American Women? Catherine East. Southern Newspaper Publishers Association Foundation, 1970.

"Your Money and Your Future," Chase Manhattan Bank, 1969.

ON LEISURE AND RETIREMENT

4 days, 40 hours, edited by Riva Poor. Bursk & Poor, 1970.

Helpful Hints on Managing Your Money for Retirement, William Laas. Popular Library, 1970.

How to Find Leisure Time and Use It Creatively, A Guide for the Busy Woman, Lucile Rood. Dorrance, 1968.

The Psychological Aspects of Retirement, Harold Geist, Ph. D. Charles C. Thomas, 1968.

"Your Retirement," Institute of Life Insurance, 277 Park Avenue, New York, N. Y. 10017.

ON THE WORLD OF WORK

Creative Careers for Women, Joan Scobey and Lee Parr McGrath. Simon & Schuster, 1968.

From Kitchen to Career, Adele Lewis and Edith Bobroff. Bobbs-Merrill, 1965.

How to Start a Profitable Retirement Business, Arthur Liebers. Pilot Books, 1968.

"Job-Finding Techniques for the Mature Woman,"

Women's Bureau. Superintendent of Documents, U.S. Government Printing Office, Washington, D.C. 20402 (30 cents).

So You Want to Be a Working Mother, Lois Benjamin. Funk & Wagnalls, 1966.

"Starting and Managing a Small Business of Your Own." Superintendent of Documents, U.S. Government Printing Office, Washington, D.C. 20402 (25 cents).

380 Part-Time Jobs for Women, Ruth Lembeck. Dell, 1968.

Women at Work—Every Woman's Guide to Successful Employment, Elmer Winter. Simon & Schuster, 1967.

Women! Business Needs You!, Sabatino A. Russo, Jr., and William Laas. Popular Library, 1968.

Work When You Want to Work, John Fanning. Macmillan, 1969.

INDEX